Winning Is Everything
and Other American Myths

Winning Is Everything and Other American Myths

Thomas Tutko
and William Bruns

MACMILLAN PUBLISHING CO., INC.

NEW YORK

Macmillan Publishing Co., Inc.
866 Third Avenue, New York, N.Y. 10022
Collier Macmillan Canada, Ltd.

Library of Congress Cataloging in Publication Data

Tutko, Thomas A
    Winning is everything and other American myths.

    Includes index.
    1. Sports—Philosophy. 2. Sports for children.
I. Bruns, William, joint author. II. Title.
GV706.T87   796'.019'22   75–45325
ISBN 0–02–620770–2

FIRST PRINTING 1976

Printed in the United States of America

GV
706
.T87

Contents

Introduction

OVER THE PAST fifteen years there has been a growing and disturbing preoccupation in this country with professional sports. New leagues challenge old leagues, spawning more teams, more expansion, and fresh crops of self-seeking superstars. Owners move about the countryside, leaving few cities unturned in their search for eager fans who will pay higher prices for a cheaper product. So many team nicknames have been appropriated that skunks, rats, weasels, piranhas, and vultures may one day grace the back of team uniforms—appropriately so, some critics would argue.

Obsessive as we have become in cultivating our spectator sports, I believe a much more destructive craze is the prevailing competitive ethic: Winning is everything. . . . You are nothing until you are Number One. . . . Don't tell us how you played the game; did you win? . . . Are you willing to pay the price to keep winning? This win-at-all-costs mania long ago seized high-level collegiate sports (helping to bring about deficits in the athletic departments at nearly every major university), but even more unfortunate is the fact that it is steadily engulfing children's sports.

We organize children's leagues, give them uniforms, hand out trophies, set up play-offs and All-Star teams, send them to "bowl" games, and encourage them to compete at earlier and earlier ages. In the eyes of many parents and coaches, it's apparently never too early to get a jump on the family next door, the pros, or the Russians. Track and field records include those for "athletes" as young as one; three-year-olds compete in the baton-twirling "Olympics" every year; hockey leagues are enlisting four-year-olds; and minibike racers can compete in national championships at the age of six.

By the time he is eight, the enterprising young athlete—given properly "motivated" parents and a sturdy family car—can compete in organized sports nearly fifty-two weeks a year. No matter whether he lives in Seattle, San Diego, Miami, Boston, or St. Louis, he can start with Pop Warner football or soccer in the fall, move over to basketball or ice hockey in the winter, and turn to Little League baseball in the spring and early summer—assuming, of course, that he's not already tied up with swimming, tennis, golf, track, gymnastics, skiing, figure skating, or speed skating. During the "off-season," or what is left of it, the young athlete can join his family on a vacation that, in many cases, has been wedged in between play-offs in one sport and sign-ups for another. Or he (and increasingly she) can choose from among thousands of summer sports camps that are proliferating at college campuses across the country.

If we continue to feed this compulsion to succeed in sports, I'm convinced that someone, someday, will try to organize a Pee Wee Olympics for athletes ten and under. The promoter could fill the stands with parents and relatives, charge entry fees, and have a financial success. Some individuals would consider this as simply a "lark," a few parents having fun. To some degree this may be true. But we need to consider the child's point of view. Clearly, the message to him, if only on a fun level, is to compete, to be Number One, to set a record. The die is being cast whether the parents are fully aware of it or not.

Many people would argue that this should be the purpose of sports—to strive for records, championships, Olympic teams, and professional careers. But how many million youngsters are we sacrificing along the way so that ten players can entertain us in a pro basketball game? How many people are we eliminating who love sports but who never make the team because they're not going to be a "winner"—they're too short or too slow or too weak. Everybody is preoccupied with "Who won?" I'm concerned with how many good athletes have been scarred by injury or burned out psychologically by the time they were fifteen because they were unable to meet the insatiable needs of their parents, their coach, their fans, or their own personal obsession, or who are rejected and made to feel ashamed of having limited athletic prowess. As Joe Paterno, one of college football's most successful head coaches, has said, "It's time we let kids grow up naturally. Suppose they don't grow up to be athletic superstars. That isn't so terrible. Let them find their own interests and their own levels. Let them be kids instead of forcing them to play at being adults." Even a number of pro athletes are repelled by the excesses they see in kids' sports. Star fullback Larry Csonka, for example, is against the idea of midget football, and will not let his two sons play. "Take a little kid, put him under the pressure of a big championship game before his parents and his entire world, and it can be very bad for him," said Csonka. "Especially if he loses. The whole country loves football, and so do I. But parents don't stop to consider all the things that can go wrong for a young fellow pushed into that kind of pressure."

This is what is painful to me—to see the healthy, positive benefits that sports can impart to a youngster being subverted by the belief that unless you are a winner you can never be truly happy or satisfied with yourself. This competitive thirst may produce Olympic champions and Super Bowl winners; it

is even understandable at the professional level, where winning
is the bottom line question: "If I don't win I lose my job, and
my job is everything to me. It is my livelihood." But the reality
of the situation is this: over 5,000,000 preadolescent boys and
girls competed in organized sports in 1975, but *less than one
percent* of them will ever sign a pro contract or make a U.S.
team in a sport like swimming or gymnastics. The great
majority of young athletes are competing in a sport because
they want to have fun, want to improve their skills, and want
to be with their friends. Yet many of their parents believe that
they should raise their young athletes the way Vince Lombardi
ran his football team. These parents are sucked in by the
glamour and the myths that help perpetuate American sports.
They are seduced by athletic scholarships, pro bonuses,
$400,000 contracts, notoriety, and the belief that striving for
Number One is what makes America great. But they fail to
realize that even among those who reach the top, there is a
great amount of pain, misery, frustration, and anxiety.

In hopes that everybody involved in youth sports will step
back and get a perspective on what is happening, I will look at
the child in sports from four main viewpoints.

1. In the opening chapters I will explore the underlying
beliefs—or myths—of American sports: clichés such as "Sports
build character" and "Competition brings out the best in
man," as well as our notions about the virtues of winning and
the horrors of losing.

Don't get me wrong. I'm not against sports. I believe
athletics can provide the greatest area for potential growth in
our educational system. They can also be used as a very
effective medium to develop family communication. Secondly,
I'm not against sensibly run leagues for children. A well-
organized league with good coaching can help more youngsters participate more often. It's when we overorganize, make
every move, don't allow the children a voice, and only permit
them to play out a role that we stifle their creative, energetic
potential. Third, I'm not against professionalism—if it is

viewed solely as entertainment and not as a way of life to be emulated by young people. And fourth, I'm all in favor of competition and the *striving* to win. Competition is an integral part of American life. It can provide joy and excitement and help us probe our limits and our capacities. It's HOW we're competing that's all wrong. Even down at the Pop Warner football and Little League baseball level we play with only one real objective, and that is to win. I'm against insanity in athletics, and many of our attitudes border on the disturbed.

2. If parents are going to allow their children to get involved in high-pressure sports during the preadolescent years, then I feel it is imperative that they oversee what is happening. The coach, the league, the pressure, the push may all be very destructive. Winning at all costs is a very narrow-minded, shortsighted approach to life. It gives us only a temporary glance, not the total perspective. We miss the forest for the trees. We are preoccupied with the moment of winning and we fail to observe the long-range destruction.

The effects may not be physically evident (although the damage to a growing body is a constant danger—see chapter 11 on sports injuries). Nobody may be able to point a finger and say, "Here's where sports hurt Johnny." But failure in sports, or heavy-handed approaches by parents and coaches can destroy a child's self-esteem, turn him away from a lifelong involvement in physical activity, foster negative attitudes towards authority figures, and encourage hostile, aggressive behavior. Parents simply can't assume that every coach is worried more about the welfare of his athletes than about the outcome of the game, that winning automatically brings about positive changes and long-range personality benefits, or even that participation in sports will make people happy. Even if the athlete has talent or is playing on a winning team, there's no guarantee that—given a free choice—he will automatically want to go out for the same sport the following season.

I've found that many parents seem to think that dealing with their child as an athlete is somehow isolated from the rest of child rearing. They believe that the father and the coach can teach the techniques and that the emotions will take care of themselves. Indeed, most how-to-raise-children books fail to devote even a chapter to organized sports, thus ignoring what can be a crucial influence on a child's physical and emotional development. For parents—and coaches—to assume that youngsters are not affected by losing or getting hit by the ball or not being on a winning team or riding the bench is not only naïve but unfair to the child's sensitivities. We're thrusting them into an environment that is relatively vicious, and many of them are not ready for it. As Vic Braden, the prominent California tennis coach and a fellow psychologist, says, "A youngster can get ruined in a math class and get ruined by a coach on the athletic field. But to me, the damage in sports is worse than anything I've ever seen." He points out that American society has tied sports so closely to masculinity and virility that the boy who fails to make the team or is ridiculed by his gym teacher for being clumsy can suffer severe psychological problems unless he is bolstered by sympathetic parents. Such youngsters often just turn their backs on competitive sports and the benefits of a physically active life.

Throughout the book, I discuss many of these psychological nuances. I also suggest ways in which parents and coaches can help youngsters handle the emotions of sports. My emphasis is on the preadolescent, pre-high school athlete—both boys and girls—but the philosophies expressed and the approaches recommended remain just as important as the athlete advances up through the scholastic and collegiate ranks into the pros. The intensity of competition increases as the focus narrows solely to winning, yet the qualities of sensitivity and awareness are no less vital. They are simply overlooked or ignored by many "big-time" coaches and managers.

3. However enlightened parents might be in their approach to childhood sports, many of their efforts can be undermined by an ineffective coach, one who is more concerned about winning than about the sensitivities of his players, a hard-nosed

"competitor" who has to be forced by league rules to play every youngster in every game. On the other hand, an effective coach—one whose goal is not so much to win more games as to develop players who are happy, well-adjusted human beings—can be a third parent, a crucial influence on impressionable psyches.

In view of these powerful influences, a long section is devoted to those who coach on the preadolescent level—from their psychological warfare with parents to the pressures on them to deal with the physical and emotional growth of their players. I will discuss many of the problems faced by coaches at this level, and suggest methods of building coach-athlete and coach-parent communication that will enable the coach to deal more effectively with his job.

4. Surrounded by an all-encompassing competitive mania, where simply participating and having fun no longer seem to be the goal in many leagues, what can parents and coaches do to bring a new perspective to childhood sports? The final chapter will discuss alternate models to the insanity, some of which are already being effectively employed here and in Canada. The aim should be for everyone involved in youth sports—parents, coaches, and league officials—to redirect their goals away from the final score and final standings. Winning should not be the score or the results of a race but each youngster working to his or her maximum potential. The idea should be to encourage physical activity by every child, not to weed out those who are uncoordinated or untalented. Let's compete, let's play to win—but let's keep it all in perspective. Young athletes should see the thrill of competing, not simply winning; they should be judged by their effort, not just the end results or lack of results. As Los Angeles relief pitcher Mike Marshall, a kinesiology professor in the off-season and an independent spirit, puts it, "Our whole society is deluged with the concept that winning is all that's important. That is bull. All that's important is that the individual does the best he can. Victory does not elate me, nor does defeat depress me. The

only victory for me is the quality of the competition, not the final score."

The more we make sports a life-and-death matter and the more we concentrate on a youngster's needing to win or to succeed in order to feel worthwhile, the more we will undermine the contribution that sports can make. Let's eliminate the grandiosity of sports and see it for what it should offer to ninety-nine percent of those who participate: healthy recreation, where a child can have fun while developing physical skills and emotional maturity in a positive interaction with other children. Let's teach young athletes the fundamentals, talk to them about their batting averages and field goal percentages, and take pride in their triumphs. But let's not neglect or abuse their motivations and emotions. Let's not forget that when they pull on a uniform, they are still children, not miniature adults.

Winning Is Everything
and Other American Myths

1

To Win or Not to Win: That Is the Question

ONE EFFECT OF this country's sports craze is that owners, coaches, players, and fans all suffer from the same delusions. We thirst for whatever tangible evidence we can find that says, "We're a winner. We're Number One!" The athlete or coach who is near the bottom always feels, "I'll win and that'll mean something. I'll be worthwhile, loved, honored, and obeyed." This fundamental faith in the goodness of sports was typified by George Raveling when he took over as head basketball coach at Washington State in 1972 with the goal of helping to end UCLA's dominance in the Pacific Eight conference and in the country. When Raveling was asked how he thought he could succeed where so many had fallen short before, he answered: "I just rely on that saying that the struggle to the top is a rugged one but the view from the top is beautiful. I want that view, and we'll work as hard as we can to get there."

I like Raveling; I think he's a model young coach. But what realistically will happen if, by chance, he knocks off UCLA in

1

1982 and wins the NCAA title? What happens when *anybody* reaches the top in sports? Can they relax and savor that moment? Of course not. They have to do it again the next year, and the year after that. When the San Francisco Warriors won the NBA title in 1975, a newspaper headline the next afternoon read: "Are the Warriors Going to be One Year Champions?" No longer is it even, "Did you win?" but "How long are you going to keep winning?" Even if you are John Wooden and you win seven consecutive NCAA championships, your fans grumble when you fail to win an eighth. In individual sports like swimming and track and field, breaking records only leaves new records to be broken. No matter at what level we compete and in whatever sport, when we attain a goal we simply move it up another notch, hunting for a perfection that is always just out of reach.

Winning, in fact, is like drinking salt water; it will never quench your thirst. It is an insatiable greed. There are never enough victories, never enough championships or records. If we win, we take another gulp and have even greater fantasies.

From their inception in 1960, the Dallas Cowboys went twelve frustrating years without winning the National Football League championship. They had outstanding talent and they came close on several occasions, but they never could win "the big one." When they finally did win the Super Bowl in 1972, owner Tex Schramm went on television in the midst of his celebrating players and boasted that Dallas would now build a *dynasty!* That's what happens when you drink salt water instead of champagne.

Individual athletes are caught up in the same competitive madness. In 1974, 22-year-old Jimmy Connors suddenly blasted his way to the top of the tennis world by winning Wimbledon and Forest Hills and over $200,000. By September there was no denying his number one ranking. Yet he was never able to relax and enjoy his time on top, something he had trained for from the time he was three years old. A week after winning at Forest Hills he won a tournament in Los Angeles and then was practically forced into playing in San Francisco, two nights later. Furthermore, reporters began asking him what he would do for an encore in 1975. "Well, I plan to just have another great year," he told them. "Do it all over again. Pancho Gonzales told me the other day, 'Jim, you proved this year you're a *good* player. But you'll have to do it a lot of times to prove you're a great one.' "

Added one of Connors' tennis rivals, Alex Mayer: "You have to say he's at a peak. The question now is can he stay there. To be immortalized, he has to keep winning."

Freud would have clearly defined our behavior as a repetition compulsion because there is no moment where the winning can feel, "I've made it." In *Meat on the Hoof*, Texas football player Gary Shaw wrote: "A clear-cut victory leads only to another challenge in a perpetual rat race. As long as there is an attempt to hold on to this simple view of life as a series of challenges and victories with a few winners and many losers, then we will be trapped in an anxious and basically frustrating existence."

In pro football, the elation of a Sunday victory might last until Monday morning. But then the coach and his players begin to worry about next Sunday's game. Counting exhibition games and the play-offs, a team can be consumed by Sunday preparation for nearly six months. Is it any wonder most head coaches seem preoccupied? Only one—the Super Bowl winner—is allowed to be happy for the other six months of the year. Even then, a coach like Don Shula, whose Miami Dolphins were winners in 1973 and 1974, is never allowed to be content where he is. He must set new goals: "We can't rest on our laurels; we want to win three in a row. No other team has ever done that." I can't blame Shula for challenging a team that had already enjoyed extraordinary success. But the point is that two straight Super Bowl victories are really only temporary in his mind. There has to be a third.

Let's speculate for a moment. What if Shula, before the 1974–75 season, had told reporters: "We're not really worrying about winning the title this year. We're still enjoying last year"? Not only would his sanity have been questioned, he would have been investigated by a Senate subcommittee on insatiable competitiveness.

The craze in this country that demands that your success in sports is measured only by winning, that you are nothing until you're Number One, was crystallized by Vince Lombardi's dictum "Winning isn't everything. It's the only thing." Years later, the famous football coach claimed he had been misquoted, that what he had actually said was, "Winning is not everything—but making the effort to win is."

In fact, the "winning" quote apparently originated with another football coach, the late Red Sanders, when he was at Vanderbilt in 1940. The phrase later surfaced, inevitably, in a John Wayne movie, *Trouble Along the Way*. Wayne plays a tough ex-professional football coach who is trying to keep custody of his only daughter while at the same time whipping a small college team into a national powerhouse. Donna Reed, an employee of the child welfare bureau, asks him one day, "Is winning everything to you?" The Duke replies, "No, ma'am. Winning isn't everything. It's the only thing."

This drive to compete and to be a "winner" has always been part of the American psyche. Our early ancestors were aggressive and competitive to begin with. They knew they were pitted against amazing odds, but they also felt they were a select and chosen group. They defied their mother country and were successful. Later came the "frontier spirit," the belief in survival of the fittest, and the growing American fetish for figures, statistics, records, and winners. Over forty years ago, John R. Tunis wrote, in *The American Way in Sport*: "We worship the victors. But why? The Dutch don't especially, nor the Swedes, neither do the Danes, the Swiss, or the English, and they all seem fairly civilized people." We devised an international "scoreboard" to chart our successes in the

Olympics as well as in our wars, an obsession that was tragically reflected in our approach to Vietnam, where both President Johnson and President Nixon vowed that they were not going down in history as "the first American President who lost a war."

The competitive instinct that permeates the American spirit is one of the most highly prized values in the country, emanating from our presidents on down. But it is not just competition that is important—it is who *wins* that really matters. When Gerald Ford was vice-president, he wrote in *Sports Illustrated*: "It has been said that we are losing our competitive spirit in this country, the thing that made us great, the guts of the free-enterprise system. I don't agree with that; the competitive urge is deep-rooted in the American character." Fair enough, but then he goes on to say: "We have been asked to swallow a lot of home-cooked psychology in recent years that winning isn't all that important anymore, whether on the athletic field or in any other field, national and international. I don't buy that for a minute. It is not enough to just compete. Winning is very important. Maybe more important than ever." Later, when he was president, Ford continued to plug winning as a great American tradition. "What about winning?" he asked. "How about a good word for the ultimate reason any of us have for going into a competitive sport? As much as I enjoyed the physical and emotional dividends that college athletics brought me, I sincerely doubt if I ever suited up, put on my helmet . . . without the total commitment of going out there to win, not to get exercise, gold or glory, but simply to win."

President Ford is just one of many defenders of the winning creed, as the following quotations will show.

Washington Redskins coach George Allen: "The winner is the only individual who is truly alive. I've said this to our ball club: 'Every time you win, you're reborn; when you lose, you die a little.' " (Allen has a career won-lost record that most coaches would envy. But by his own definition he is a loser, because although he has made the play-offs six times, he has failed to win the Super Bowl.)

Texas football coach Darrell Royal: "The only way I know how to keep football fun is to win. That's the only answer. There is no laughter in losing." (Read *Meat on the Hoof* to confirm that Royal is not joking.)

Former Kansas City Chiefs coach Hank Stram: "It's only a game when you win. When you lose it's hell." (Especially when it costs you your job.)

Former Boston Bruins coach Bep Guidolin: "Winning is the name of the game. The more you win the less you get fired." (This statement was made before Guidolin lost his job when his Bruins lost in the seventh game of the 1974 Stanley Cup play-off finals to Philadelphia.)

Alabama football coach Bear Bryant, asked what he most wanted to be remembered for: "I'd like if it'd be for winning. . . . That's our approach: If it's worth playing, it's worth paying the price to win."

Ohio State coach Woody Hayes: "Winners are men who have dedicated their whole lives to winning." (That's why you don't find Ohio State playing Alabama.)

Dallas quarterback Roger Staubach: "In pro football winning is all there is. If you don't win, you haven't done what the game is about." (Staubach is an active member of the Fellowship for Christian Athletes. Does he feel that Christ was a winner or a loser?)

Norman Vincent Peale: "I once asked Ty Cobb, 'Why do you put such an emphasis on winning? It's only a game.' He said, 'That's the reason I'm out there. Why play if you don't play to win?' " (What about camaraderie and the joy of simply playing a game?)

Baseball manager Billy Martin: "The players may not like you some of the time but I've always made the statement I'd play Adolf Hitler to win." (Yes, but Hitler was a loser.)

Pro basketball guard Pete Maravich: "Personal things like

leading the league [in scoring] don't get you a cup of coffee. My obsession is to be on a championship team. As soon as I am, I'll retire. Definitely. Right then. Because then I will have been successful. I'm really only happy when I'm winning. Losses always bother me." (Playing for an expansion team in New Orleans, he should enjoy a long, unhappy career.)

Hubert Humphrey, in the Minnesota Vikings dressing room, after a club official pointed out he never shows up after a losing game: "That's true. Frankly, I love being around winners. When you win, you win. And when you lose, you lose. And winning is a lot more fun."

Why has winning taken on such importance? Why have we become obsessed with winning at all costs? For one thing, we play our games against the backdrop of an intensely competitive culture. A high premium is placed on achievement and success. Americans measure everything in terms of progress, or pseudo progress; we always have to feel that we're moving up. In a society that is preoccupied with competition, the average person needs something to latch on to that says, "I'm really *worthwhile*, too." Winning can provide that boost, even if it means that a person is living vicariously through a sports team like the old Green Bay Packers or basking in the triumphs of a once-heroic Arnold Palmer.

Secondly, we are heirs to the Judeo-Christian ethic, which states in principle that man should work hard to succeed, that if a person does his best, works unceasingly, and makes the right sacrifices, he will win. The assumption is that somehow the winner does everything right and the loser does everything wrong. All too often, the message that comes through to those who lose or who fail to reach the top is that obviously they didn't work hard enough and that they're not as worthwhile as the winners. Our tendency is to excuse the shortcomings of a winner—to gloss over his human frailties. But when a person starts to lose, we begin to question his character. Winners and losers are actually seen as good and bad people. If the athlete manifests certain behavior that leads to success, we say he has "courage," he's a "competitor," he's "mentally tough." Those who fail to demonstrate the same behavior are "losers," "flakes," "gutless," or "chokers." Our winning sports heroes even begin to appear sexually superior; they are "better looking" and more appealing. Their faces sell products on television, although it's interesting to note that the faces change as the level of success changes.

A study by one of my students, Seth Brody, clearly supports the "halo effect" of winners. Individuals were asked to make personality ratings of amateur boxers viewed on film. The winner was seen as more mature, better looking, more valuable, more potent, and more active than the loser. These findings are reinforced by successful sports figures who are quoted in newspapers and magazines. For example, Pete Newell, general manager of the Los Angeles Lakers, commented on Oregon coach Dick Harter and his efforts to produce a team that could end the UCLA basketball dynasty: "I'm encouraged to see young men go through the demanding process of building a winner. You make it and you look around at the others who have made it and you say, 'He's a man, and I'm a man.' It can be an educating experience."

Perhaps we could justify this obsession with winning if, at the end of the road, it led to a better and a more wholesome life. If when you won a trophy or the championship or set a record, you became a more contented person. Or people used you as a mature model. Or something meaningful happened to you beyond making $100,000 a year and being in demand on the meat loaf circuit. Unfortunately, when you finally do win the whole ball of wax, not only do you have to win it again, but you become a marked man. Everybody wants to beat you. You accumulate enemies simply because you have won. When U.S. backstroke swimmer John Naber handed East Germany's Roland Matthes his first defeat in seven years, Naber acknowledged his dilemma: "I wanted his record more than anything.

Now all I'll get is the headache of people trying to beat me simply because I was the one who beat him."

Countless other athletes have struggled to the top only to find that winning is a hollow trip. In fact, the higher up the scale they go, the worse the pressures become: the incredible strain to keep winning; the clamoring public that demands autographs; banquet appearances and business deals; the insatiable news media that hunger for "fresh" quotes and every possible insight into the athlete's personal life; and the athlete's own internal demands to maintain the conditioning and training that brought him to the top in the first place. Small wonder that many top athletes finally confide, "What the hell is it all about?" Said tennis heroine Chris Evert: "It's tough being on top. It's lonely there. It's lonely because the other players are so competitive. If you want to be the best, you can't be best friends with everybody."

Another contributing pressure is the realization that an athlete can be a winner one day and a complete bum the next. Unless he is consistent, he runs the risk of being classified as a loser and facing the wrath of all his "loyal" fans. Ferguson Jenkins won 20 games or more for seven consecutive seasons. When he finally came up short—winning "only" 14 games in 1973—his fans in Chicago started booing him, and his owner proceeded to trade him to one of the worst teams in baseball (where, ironically, he won 25 games the following season).

The final irony is that if an athlete or a team wins *too* consistently, many of their fans will start getting bored if records are not broken or the winning margin is not overwhelming. Let a team win too much, like the New York Yankees of old or the UCLA basketball team, and many people are unhappy—from the critics who lament, "Break up the dynasty! They're ruining the game" to disgruntled players who have to ride the bench when they could be starting on any other team. Fans begin to form a strange alliance. It is not that they are *for* a team but against the other team. I know a number of basketball fans who are clearly against UCLA whenever they play, simply because they win too often. Even when John Wooden was in the midst of UCLA's 88-game winning streak, he and his wife, Nell, found very little contentment. More often it was a life of aggravation and smoldering pressure. Late in the streak, Mrs. Wooden told a reporter:

These should have been the best years of our lives. But they haven't been. Nine national championships in ten years is great. So are the winning streaks. But the fans are so greedy. They've reached the point where they are unhappy if John wins a championship game by five points. If he ever loses a game they're going to say that he's too old and he's lost his touch. They can stretch the rules and let him stay until he's sixty-seven, but I wonder if it would be worth it. What more does my husband have to prove?

The UCLA fans were indeed voracious winners. Yet by this stage in John Wooden's career, his own drive for success had become an obsession. Four months later, after UCLA had been upset by North Carolina State in the NCAA finals, Wooden made an unprecedented three recruiting trips to Salt Lake City in order to finally tie down seven-foot Brett Vroman, a player he felt the Bruins needed to win even more championships in the coming years. Here was the greatest basketball coach in college history, a 64-year-old man with a heart problem, pursuing a 17-year-old hotshot who might help keep a basketball machine humming for another three or four years. Is any clearer testimony needed to show us where our fanaticism has brought us?

2

Symptoms of a Winning Craze

THOSE WHO LIVE blindly by the ethic "Win-at-all-costs" need to step back and honestly ask themselves, "Why? What are we trying to accomplish? What is sports really contributing?" Because, objectively speaking, the competitive standards that rule professional and collegiate sports today are producing far more "losers" than "winners."

One team wins the Super Bowl while 25 other clubs cry "Shut up and deal." There's one World Series winner and 23 teams that hope for renewal in spring training. One team wins the Stanley Cup, leaving 17 disgruntled losers. Out of over 135 professional teams that crisscross the country in pursuit of the brass ring, only eight bring back a championship. In individual sports like golf and tennis, just one winner emerges from a field that can number hundreds. Even winners are losers, and losers can be winners. The 1974 Cincinnati Reds had the *second-best record* in baseball, yet they failed even to make the play-offs; they finished second in their division behind Los Angeles. Meanwhile, a losing team in the regular

11

season could make the playoffs by winning its division and
then proceed to win the championship. The line between a
winner and a loser is often so thin that it may simply represent
chance, as opposed to skill and determination. It may simply be
luck, over which we have no control. Reducing further the
elite corps of annual winners is the overlap of those who win
two or three years in succession—the Oaklands in baseball, the
Miamis in football, the Philadelphias in hockey, etc.

Pressured from all sides by such statistics and the unrelenting demands to become a winner (and further exacerbated by
the enormous amounts of money at stake), is it any wonder
that the sports field is overrun with neurotic behavior, acts of
violence, and outright greed? Or that pro athletes can flaunt
long-held virtues such as loyalty, sportsmanship, and altruism
with near impunity? We'll tolerate almost anything in the
name of winning—cruelty, insensitivity, drugs, cheating, and
lying—as long as the winners don't get caught. Even the sports
pages, once a haven from the ugly realities headlined elsewhere
in the newspaper, now read like a scandal sheet—exposés,
fights, sexual exploits, strikes, racism, recruiting abuses, verbal
assaults, accusations. The long-treasured belief that "Competition brings out the best in man" is clearly a bizarre one in light
of what is happening. The reverse is increasingly the case:
competition brings out the worst in man.

To some people these are isolated problems or the reflection
of a society that has dumped its ailments on the sports world. I
view them as symptoms of a competitive spirit that is wildly
out of control and has lost all perspective. When competitive
dreams, ambitions, drives, and ultimate financial reward clash
with reality, when there are desperate, compulsive efforts to be
successful in a society that offers little sympathy for losers,
symptoms are going to occur. These symptoms result from
three different, though sometimes interrelated, pressures:

First, there are the actions that occur basically because
people want to become a winner, e.g., the use of drugs,
neurotic work habits, cheating, lying—anything that will help

you become a winner or build up hopes of winning. Violence and aggression are seen as important qualities in the drive to reach the top. In hockey, for instance, there is the feeling by many that you cannot be a big winner unless you have players who love to use roughhouse tactics such as fighting and intimidation, as the Boston Bruins and the Philadelphia Flyers have proved in recent years.

Secondly, there are the frustrations of not winning—on-the-field brawls, locker room fights, bickering, backbiting, disloyalty—indulged in by supposedly mature adult models. When athletes and coaches are placed in a frustrating, almost impossible situation—"win-or-else" despite the odds against them—feelings of futility are bound to manifest themselves.

Thirdly, there are the actions undertaken to perpetuate winning, such as recruiting violations and cheating, as well as the reactions to being on top, with its seductions, adulation, money, and pampering of egos, all of which lead to the greed, narcissism, and superstar antics that plague sports today. Intrateam squabbles and fisticuffs can also occur on a winning team—notably the Oakland Athletics—but ironically this is seen as a valuable ingredient in the team's "character."

Intertwined with these symptoms are the plain realities of high-voltage competition. Athletes are put under an incredible amount of pressure to produce in a limited amount of time. Not only that, they are judged and criticized by fans whose will-of-the-wisp loyalties are about as fragile as the last victory. Few of us live under that kind of pressure. Thus, every personality in sports—no matter how successful and self-secure the athlete might be—is bound to show some symptoms of strain over a period of time.

Following, in more detail, are the major symptoms of the win-at-all-costs sickness at the professional and collegiate level—which, not incidentally, are the models for our young athletes.

Drugs

The use of drugs in sports—to get "up" for a game or to become a better athlete—stems not only from society's pressure to win but also from the influence of our drug culture. Everybody is looking for the elixir. If you are a loser, you want to be a winner, so you try drugs, even though a government commission report and other medical studies report no evidence that drugs increase performance. "There is no good scientific evidence that any of these substances really helps," said Dr. Donald L. Cooper, an Oklahoma State University physician. He thinks it's futile to take urine tests of Olympic winners, arguing that it's most often the losers and also-rans—not the winners—who have taken drugs. "When only winners are tested," he said, "the implication arises that there is some relationship between winning and doping, while in reality the opposite has been found to be true."

What may in fact be happening is that the athlete who uses drugs may view his performance from a different perspective. A number of drug studies show that although performances may remain the same or even decrease, an athlete under the influence of drugs thinks that he is stronger and more combative, and thus more effective. In other words, the subjective report that the athlete feels he is doing well does not coincide with the objective report that there is no improvement. The conclusion is that the benefits are psychological. Football linebacker Steve Kiner, who admitted to using drugs all through college and during his first four years in the pros, observed that the constant drug highs finally began chipping away at his physical condition. "I was dilapidated," he said. "You can burn yourself out on drugs without even realizing it. My weight went down to 185 [from 215]. I felt I was still in great shape, when I wasn't."

If, indeed, there are benefits psychologically, then the drug user cheats himself out of the experience of going through competition on his own. It is as if the drug did it, and thus he feels left out, as if he did not experience the event by himself. The athlete may begin to trust his drugs more than his own body, especially if he feels they enhance his performance. "You begin to think you would lose the game if you hadn't taken the pill," said John Brodie, the former San Francisco quarterback. "You think you can't perform as well without them."

In addition to the potential physical abuse involved in using drugs, there is an important philosophical question. Dr. Robert Kerlan, the medical director of the National Athletic Health Institute in Los Angeles, argues: "The essence of sports is matching the natural ability of men. When you start using drugs, money, or anything else surreptitiously to gain an unnatural advantage, you have corrupted the purpose of sports as well as the individuals involved in the practice."

The Glorification of Violence

It is one thing to accept tough physical contact and the rites of intimidation as an accepted part of sports, notably football and hockey—but quite another to *welcome* fighting as a motivational tool, or to defend violence in general as "crowd-pleasing" and "part of the game." Yet that is what we are doing in sports today.

Midway through the 1974 baseball season, the Pittsburgh Pirates and the Cincinnati Reds engaged in a bench-clearing brawl that Pirates manager Danny Murtaugh called "one of the best in a long time." The donnybrook seemed to wake up the slumping Pirates and they went on a month-long rampage that vaulted them into first place. "That fight could have been the game that finally brought togetherness to this club," noted Murtaugh, almost in appreciation. Nobody got killed in the melee, but was the behavior exhibited by these supposed models for our youngsters any different from a street fight in New York? Both acts bring solidarity to an in-group. In an article in *Atlantic Monthly*, Larry King describes the relationship between violence and character building as it relates to pro football: "Pro football is a mean game, ideally played by mean men. If it builds character, so does street mugging."

A good healthy free-for-all is also compatible with the end-justifies-the-means ideology advocated by Washington Redskins coach George Allen. After his players waged a melee with the St. Louis Cardinals during the 1973 season, Allen told a television interviewer that he "loved the fight. . . . If we didn't go out there and fight I'd be worried. You go out there and protect your teammates. The guys who sit on the bench, they're the losers. That team's losing." He recalled how he had encouraged a free-for-all in 1966 while he was coaching the Los Angeles Rams—"just to get 'em going. Just to get 'em all together. . . . Because unless you get 'em all together, unless you have that, you aren't going to be a winner. It's all part of winning." *Washington Post* writer William Gildea responded: "If a team can't be inspired within the rules, break the rules, Allen is saying. If it serves a purpose, mix in a little violence. Using a fight as an instrument of victory is a graphic and sad example of the lengths to which one obsessed with winning will go."

In hockey, meanwhile, the common rebuttal to critics of on-ice violence was supplied by Ted Lindsay, the National Hockey League's record-holder for career-penalty minutes, who said on national television: "If you don't have guts, and you can't take it, you don't belong in hockey." *New York Times* reporter Gerald Eskenazi wrote: "Presumably, some children without guts now will give up the game on Lindsay's advice. Presumably, those who remain in kids' leagues across North America will be those with guts." And in hockey "guts" means a willingness to slug it out if provoked into a fight. It doesn't mean to show courage by having the self-control and patience to stay out of a fight, but to take cheap shots, or a challenge to fight, "like a man." Retaliate with your fists and, if possible, the butt of your stick. Show that you want to be a winner and that you can't be pushed around.

The pros and cons of on-ice violence were even debated in the courtroom in 1975, when Boston's Dave Forbes was charged with aggravated assault with a dangerous weapon—his hockey stick. His victim was Henry Boucha of the Minnesota North Stars, who almost lost an eye when Forbes attacked him with his stick after they had scuffled on the ice. Forbes testified that Boucha was the real culprit, claiming that Boucha hit him with a "sucker punch" from behind, and that he felt he had to retaliate or Boucha would think "he could walk all over me." Fighting back, Forbes said, is an integral part of the game, taught to players as youngsters, and a player who doesn't fight back is an easy mark.

Boston coach Don Cherry admitted that he may have contributed to the violent outbreak by his locker room talk before the game. "The pressure was really on," he testified. "We'd been losing games. We really had to win—it was an explosive game." He said he felt his job was in jeopardy. "The pressure was on me and if the pressure is on me, it's on the players." So he told them before the game: "If you don't get going, you're all going to be gone (to the minor leagues). It has always been my philosophy to win at all costs." He later added, of course, that he didn't motivate his players to injure competitors.

Before the trial (which ended with no verdict), National Hockey League president Clarence Campbell defended fighting as "a well-established safety valve for players," and even as an essential ingredient for the economic well-being of the game. "If violence ceases to exist, it will not be the same game," he said. "Insofar as fighting is part of the show, certainly we sell it. We do not promote it. We tolerate it and we bring it under disciplinary control which we believe satisfies the public."

Yet just how meaningful are the actions that Campbell does

take? In 1974, for instance, he suspended Chicago defenseman Bill White for all of five games despite what Campbell termed "one of the most serious cases of manhandling an official that has occurred this season." White struck referee Ron Wicks on the side of the head and then wrapped an arm around Wicks's head and held him in a stranglehold, shaking him violently several times. Of course, he didn't *kill* him, but then the provocation was only a disputed goal by Atlanta. Instead of Campbell's slap on the wrist, White should have been suspended for the season; there apparently is no other way to deter abusiveness to officials. One possible approach, however, would be to have all the referees and linesmen skate to the *opposite* end of the rink when a fight breaks out. Why should they risk their necks trying to break it up? Then when the players have finished brawling, if anybody is left standing they can continue the game.

A positive contrast to Campbell's action came when J. Allan Soares was removed as Brown hockey coach after his team committed eleven fouls against Harvard and one of his players was ejected after hitting a Harvard player with his stick. Brown athletic director F. A. Geiger commented: "I have become increasingly concerned about the degeneration of conduct of our players and the atmosphere surrounding the hockey program. The program is not meeting the criterion that intercollegiate athletics should be a positive part of the educational experience at Brown."

Professional athletes, meanwhile, contribute to the perpetuation of violence with their quotes. Alex Karras, the former All-Pro defensive tackle for Detroit and the ABC *Monday Night Football* commentator, reflected in a 1974 interview:

I hated everyone on the football field, and my personality would change drastically when I got out there. And that attitude was the only thing that kept me in the league. I'm not the biggest guy—I played at about 240, which is terribly light for a tackle—but I would hurt people. . . .

I had a license to kill for 60 minutes a week. My opponents were all fair game, and when I got off the field I had no regrets. It was like going totally insane. . . . Most linemen play it like that and most of them are very tough and very sadistic. In fact, the best linemen were all sadistic. . . . They were like big docile dogs that were let loose on a football field and suddenly went crazy. Just like me.

Then there is hockey's Derek Sanderson, who has parlayed fast fists, sexual shenanigans, greed, and above-average skill into a million-dollar career. He has said:

I get bitchy when I don't play well. If I play badly, I'll pick a fight in the third period just to get in a fight. I'll break a guy's leg to win. I don't care. Afterward, I'll be able to sleep. I'll say all right, I played badly, but I won the fight, so who gives a damn?

The typical argument from those within sports is that "These guys don't really mean it—it's just rhetoric." If that is true, if they are simply talking for effect or to make "good copy," then they should be honest and tell youngsters that they're lying to the press because these young athletes coming up believe what their heroes tell them.

While athletes zonk one another in the name of good, clean competition, fans contribute their own hostilities. Hockey buffs have long distinguished themselves by showering the hockey rink with debris to protest penalties or other unpopular decisions by the officials. Even once placid baseball fans have taken to harassing unpopular players such as Cincinnati's Pete Rose by hurling epithets, fruit, and half-filled beer cans from the stands. We can only hope that such behavior reached its nadir in 1974 with the infamous Beer Night Brawl in Cleveland, when fans armed with bottles, lead pipes, and knives swarmed onto the field to attack the Texas Rangers. Miraculously, there were no serious injuries.

"Play in Pain"

The winning ethic includes the assumption that the best athletes are those who are willing to "play in pain." In the eyes of many coaches and athletes, playing while injured is a proof of courage and team loyalty, even if it might further aggravate the injury and cause permanent physical damage. "It's a great test of character if a man can play hurt," said Bill Sharman, the Los Angeles Lakers coach. "It shows what kind of competitor he is. A good, hard-nosed competitor does it." This is the kind of thinking coaches would like to instill at the pro and college level. Thus you have football players wearing casts on "hairline fractures" of the arm or hobbling on gimpy knees; basketball and baseball players performing despite pulled muscles or twisted ankles; hockey players competing with broken noses or cracked ribs. The tendency is to apply the Lombardi philosophy to the injury—ignore it, deny it, it doesn't exist—while continuing to play despite the misery. Late in the 1974 baseball pennant race, Pittsburgh outfielder Wilber Stargell was hit on the right wrist by a pitch, but he stayed in the game and contributed a key home run against St. Louis. "This time of the year you've just got to play with pain and forget about it," said Stargell. "There's no tomorrow."

Under pro football's existing credo, anything is justifiable on a Sunday afternoon, because it's all in the spirit of trying to win. The expectation is that you play hard and aggressive, and if you inflict injury, that's part of the game. Kansas City linebacker Willie Lanier once broke Fred Bilitnikoff's nose with an elbow shot seconds after the Oakland receiver had dropped a pass and the play had ended. "Freddie buckled like an empty flour sack, holding his bloody face in his hands," wrote one columnist. "It was a cheap shot—no doubt about it," charged an Oakland player. Lanier responded, "I try to play hard and aggressive. I never intend to hurt anybody. During the game we go all out. Afterward, it's forgotten. We're entertainers, performers. We're expected to play hard. Things happen. I talked to Freddie after the game—everything's okay." Bilitnikoff may breathe differently for the rest of his life, but "everything's okay." Lanier just got caught up in the emotions of the game.

Scandals and Cheating

In 1973, Frank Broyles, the football coach and athletic director at the University of Arkansas, warned his colleagues about the winning-is-everything approach to intercollegiate athletics:

> What you wind up with is a syndrome where we're destroying ourselves. . . . The coach is out to spend every dollar he can to promote his program, to recruit, to build a winner so he can fill up the seats in the stadium. He also knows if he doesn't get the best players he isn't going to win. So you have a lot of have-not teams trying to catch up with the teams that are constantly winning. The coach is trying to save his job and he'll spend every penny toward that goal.

This seemingly unbreakable cycle, coupled with rising costs and the increasing demands from women's sports and intramural programs, has brought a financial and philosophical crisis to nearly every college athletic department. "We've got to slow down this drive on the campuses to be 'Number One,' " said George Hanford, director of an academic task force that completed a six-month study of college sports in 1974. Winning depends so much on talent, he said, that "the unethical recruiting and subsidy of able young athletes continues to intensify. It prompts recruiters to falsify transcripts, coaches to get grades for their athletes in courses they never attended, alumni to give star quarterbacks automobiles, and athletic departments to use work-study funds to pay athletes for sham or nonexistent jobs."

The coach is caught between the pressures to win—to save his job—and the expectations of an athlete who may be under recruitment by dozens of schools and who has been told since his sophomore year how special he is. Texas coach Darrell Royal explained the frustration: "You're out there trying to sell yourself and your school and [the high school athlete] ain't hearing a word you're saying. All he's wondering about is when you're going to start talking money."

Religiosity

The growing number of athletes and coaches who tie religion to sports participation are seeking yet another way to gain that extra edge needed to win the game. Knute Rockne once said, "Prayers work best when players are big." Yet nearly every football team today has a team prayer before the game, as if God were somehow going to play a key role in the outcome. It is as though the Holy Trinity were sitting on the 50-yard line cheering for both sides, but would eventually like the winners just a little more because obviously that team worked harder. Since both sides pray, God must be hard put to pick the winners. Nevertheless, we end up saying, "The winners prayed." Nobody says, "The losers prayed, too."

The typical view of what it is to be a good Christian is epitomized by all that athletics seems to be exemplifying: hard work, struggling, suffering, hero worship, blind obedience, the "right" values, good people versus bad people, etc. As Gary Shaw wrote about Texas assistant coach Frank Medina, in *Meat on the Hoof*:

> To those like Medina, football had obviously become a symbol of the righteous real men of the world. He often talked of the intricate connection between being a good Christian and good football player. He claimed it was impossible to be a good football player without being a good Christian. He was sure of the connection although he never made an effort to explain it.

Tying religion to football in a positive way is simply incongruous to me. Could Christ have sanctioned this? One of the Ten Commandments is to keep the Sabbath holy. Not only do the pros play on Sunday, but they brutalize people. Nobody turns the other cheek unless he wants to get it caved in. And one of the statements you hear in the locker room after a game is, "Well, we nailed 'em to the cross."

How can religious people reconcile their beliefs with the violence in football? How can we have a minister give a prayer in the locker room before the kickoff? It's like having the priest say a few words just before the lions come out to eat the good Christians. If a minister, with clear conscience, can deliver a prayer in the locker room, if he can still feel that it's a clean slate, that he can support this, then he's out of tune. Something is wrong. All he has to do is look at the violence, the injuries, the pain-killing drugs that are used to keep a player in the game. It would be healthy if some of the leading religious figures and churches would come out and say, "Look, let's face it, a large part of sports is corrupt and we will no longer help sanction it." If those in religion were truly concerned, they would make public their revulsion at the present tactics. Even on the personal level, I would really respect a religious person who said, "I'm no longer in sports because I find that it is destroying people. In my estimation, it's certainly no longer helping people find their way."

By remaining on the sidelines, so to speak, religion is contributing to the problem. When an athlete "has religion," it helps justify his violence, it placates others, it covers up the fact that he is doing many things that are socially unacceptable. Violence and aggression are okay as long as you are religious. George Allen's approach in Washington is the perfect example. He preaches violence but he has a minister who travels with the team to lead it in prayer before and after the game. That's a total paradox, except in Allen's eyes. His "religion" is: anything goes in the pursuit of victory.

Neurotic Work Habits

I don't mean to be heavy on the Redskins coach, but there's a phantom belief, which I call the George Allen Syndrome, that no matter how hard you work, if you lose you should be working harder. If you work eight hours a day and lose the game, you should be working ten hours. And if you work ten hours and lose, you should be working twelve. You may reach the point where you are working eighteen hours a day, seven days a week, without becoming a winner, and the reason may simply be that your team is not as talented as the opponents on your schedule. Yet the faith persists that you'll never be a winner unless you work harder and harder and harder, that "hard work has its just rewards."

Ironically, if a man stands on a window ledge on the twenty-fourth floor and announces he is going to jump, we go to great lengths to try to save him. Yet a man can work himself to death in athletics, and we reward him; if he is on top we encourage him to work even *harder*. Many coaches and athletes are consumed by their sport physically and psychologically, and we not only fail to stop them, but we praise them, and set them up as models. A coach with previous heart trouble can be tempting death or an athlete can literally be shortening his life by playing with injuries, yet this is seen as a valuable attribute.

Neurotic Behavior

Some people are even willing to be hated if they can be a winner. Head coach Sid Gillman, whose San Diego Chargers once ruled the old American Football League, took a hard-hearted approach in his attempts to resurrect the lowly Houston Oilers in 1974. He told his critics, "This is a tough business. I'm not trying to win any popularity contests. They hated Lombardi, and they hate Shula and Tom Landry and all they do is win. So what is the answer? If I can win everybody can hate me. I'll give them a license to despise me if I can win."

Several weeks later Gillman released veteran center Bill Curry, who told reporters that he was concerned about the Oilers' training camp atmosphere: "The big problem I see and regret very much—because I have some very close friends on the team—is that it's a situation where winning outweighs any human aspects. There is no concern for people whatsoever. It's win at all costs even if people are humiliated publicly and careers are destroyed." As it developed, the Oilers completed a

7–7 season (after consecutive 1–13 seasons) and many of the players—at least publicly—toasted Gillman as a man who had made them "winners." Even the Associated Press noted: "This victory-starved city has gone almost berserk. . . . Instead of a Captain Bligh, Gillman is looked on now more as a Moses who has come to lead the Oilers out of the wilderness."

Egocentrism and Greed

The modern pro athlete is the logical outgrowth of the present system. From the moment we find out he is talented, we baby him, give him special privileges, and heed his many whims, to the point where he *expects* this treatment. Not only is he confident that we'll look after him, but he even believes that he is making an important contribution to society. Rarely have there been parents, teachers, or coaches who say to him, "Look, you're simply playing a game. This is entertainment." Instead, most top athletes grow up to believe that sports is an end in itself, that there's no real life after that. As golfer Frank Beard noted in his book on the pro golf tour:

The No. 1 guys have to be almost totally self-centered. They have to possess an incredible burning for success . . . they do have to stomp on people who get in their way. They have to ignore their friends and their enemies and sometimes their families, and they have to concentrate entirely upon winning, upon being No. 1. There's no other way to get to the top.

The result of this conditioning, by society and by the sport itself, is that we've developed a breed of athletes who are totally self-centered and narcissistic. They're worried about what they're going to get out of the sport rather than what they can put back. The ability to give, to share, to allow a part of themselves to be invested in somebody else, seems to be a vanishing quality among many of these athletes.

I was a great admirer of Roberto Clemente, the Pittsburgh outfielder. Even in the way he died, on a mercy flight to bring supplies to earthquake-ravaged Nicaragua, he depicted the kind of person he was, and the kind of person athletes can be. He got on a little plane, although he hated to fly, and died for people he didn't even know, in a country that wasn't even his! Instead of leaving behind a legacy of newspaper clippings and memories of his baseball heroics, he set up playgrounds and baseball fields in his home town in Puerto Rico and saw that equipment was made available for youngsters so that all of them could participate.

Unfortunately, professional sports are going in the opposite direction. Money, greed, self-absorption—that is the current life-style. The players say, "Look how important I am. I can manipulate you. You want me in the NBA? Then pay me more than the ABA." The millions become a nice figure to toss around. This grandiosity about money at all levels of professional sports is also a way of saying "I'm very valuable. I'm very worthwhile. I'm a winner."

In all fairness to the athlete, that's how society has trained him. He is carefully nurtured in a hothouse environment, seduced by the soft life and fast-moving crowds, and taken care of in such a way that he becomes very dependent. He simply assumes that things are coming to him—"Give me what I'm due." A high school athletic director in Virginia told me, "These kids are coming up and they're demanding jackets and trophies and medals, and they're not even playing. They expect that they're going to get these things just by being on the team." When the athlete reaches the pros, these beliefs are strongly reinforced by his lawyer-agent and by shortsighted owners who literally scramble to give away their money to sign top draft choices, to lure athletes away from a rival league, or to hang on to their own high-salaried players.

Even those who profess to be sickened by the absurd inflation in sports are very often contributing to that inflation. For instance, noted sports lawyer Bob Woolf admitted to a reporter: "The salary structure is wild, out of proportion, and the athletes themselves know it. It's unrealistic, ridiculous.

Money has now become the name of the game, completely."
But then he went on: "Who is worth $400,000 a year coming
out of college? Maybe even $120,000 isn't realistic. But if
that's what the fair market value is, that's what the player has a
right to demand."

A perfect example of this mania is Woolf's former client,
Marvin Barnes, the second player chosen in the 1974 pro
basketball draft, who announced that he wouldn't take a penny
under $1 million. "I'd rather work in a factory than take less,"
he said arrogantly. Barnes was a player with undeniable ability,
but it was this basketball reputation that also helped him escape
with a two-year unsupervised probationary sentence for
allegedly striking a college teammate over the head with a
piece of pipe. Nevertheless, a winning basketball team was first
priority in the eyes of the St. Louis owner of the ABA, and he
agreed to pay Barnes an estimated $2.5 million. "I'm glad to be
in the ABA," Barnes joked to reporters. "It 'saved me from a
lot of factory work." Not surprisingly, Barnes cut out on his
team for two weeks early in the season and secured another
lawyer in order to renegotiate a new contract. The old one, he
claimed, was "a ripoff." But you have to wonder, who was
ripping off whom?

In contrast to Barnes's attitude was that of North Carolina
State star David Thompson, who turned down $1 million-plus
offers to turn pro after both his sophomore and junior years.
Said Thompson, a janitor's son and one of eleven children:
"You can wear only one suit at a time, drive one car and eat
just three meals a day. What do I need with a million
dollars? . . . I love basketball; I've been playing since I was
seven, but I told myself I ought to get a college education.
That's what I want to do. I'm still young. Basketball can wait."
Baseball's Pete Rose also offers a refreshing example by the
way he approaches his $160,000-a-year contract: "I make
more money than the other guys so I'd better work a lot
harder than they do."

Another manifestation of greed appears when the athlete is

not playing on a winning team. Then the only tangible bit of evidence that he is worthwhile as an athlete is the amount of money he makes. It becomes a substitute for winning. When an athlete can see only the futility of losing week after week—especially if he's a player who could be starting elsewhere around the league and bringing home play-off and endorsement income—the only thing he can do is tell his general manager, "Hey, look, either pay me or trade me. It can't be any worse. I want the opportunity to play with a winner."

Disloyalty

Another myth that has been packed away with the Andy Hardy books is the belief that loyalty is its own reward. Most pro athletes are loyal only to themselves, their paycheck, and winning. If the rival league will pay them more money, they'll jump as soon as their contract allows, if not sooner—but not without giving their team a chance to join in the bidding. This has led to the fine art of renegotiating contracts. Athletes and their lawyer-agents supposedly make a long-term commitment to the team by signing fat, multi-year contracts "for security." But let the athlete suddenly have a big season, and he wants to tear up the old contract and renegotiate. If the club won't meet his demands—"give me more or else"—he holds out or begins dickering with the other league. Curiously, these athletes leave no room for downward renegotiation after a poor season. Their "trip" is along a one-way highway, always leading to fatter paychecks and fancier fringe benefits. Fortunately, there are exceptions, like superstar pitcher Nolan Ryan. In 1973 he pitched two no-hitters and barely missed a third, yet he refused to ask for a salary increase at midseason. "They didn't try to cut my pay when I was going bad, did they?" he asked.

I feel that athletes who play out their options in an effort to force their trade to a winning team are being disloyal. The athlete's message is: "I've got to play on a team that's going to win, otherwise there's no sense in playing." He fails to meet his responsibility. Just as guilty, of course, are those club owners who threaten to move the franchise unless the fans start showing the proper "loyalty" by shelling out thirty dollars to bring the family out to a game featuring two expansion teams. An owner like Charles Finley of the Oakland A's shows loyalty to no one. He often unloads his employees— ball players as well as front-office personnel—on the slightest whim, as if they were cattle on his farm in La Porte, Indiana.

The Inability to Handle Defeat

Losing is an integral, yet badly abused, aspect of athletic competition. Losers greatly outnumber winners, and even winners stand to be losers the next day, the next week, or the next season. But nobody knows *how* to lose. We're not trained to lose, to accept limits; it's not in our sports books and it surely isn't part of our coaching philosophy. Instead, the growing tendency is a complete denial of losing. Losing is what happens to the other team, the other individual. Instead of simply admitting defeat and giving the other team or the other player due credit, sports figures feed us shoddy rationalizations and whining excuses. Defeat is invariably blamed on an outside force: they dimmed the lights every time we shot; the officials were against us; the weather was too hot, too cold, too wet, or too windy; they "tricked" us; our fans weren't behind us; the coach is playing the wrong men, he's lost communication with his players, he has a "personality problem," etc., ad nauseam. Even the game clock is sometimes a villain: "We would have won but time ran out on us."

During the 1974 World Series, in which Los Angeles lost in five quick games to Oakland, some of the Dodger players epitomized the sore loser syndrome, grumbling after every defeat that the A's were "opportunistic" and "lucky" to win. "I definitely feel we have the better team," said outfielder Bill Buckner on several occasions. "You can't fight luck." The

Oakland players, who were winning their third straight title with professional ease, were understandably perturbed by the Dodger attitude. Said outfielder Joe Rudi:

Three years ago we beat the Reds only to have them say they weren't impressed. Last year we beat the Mets and it was more of the same. Now all we've heard is how the Dodgers think we're lucky, how they think they're better, how they feel that only one or two of us would play on their team. . . . I'm very happy that they'll now have all winter to think about what we did to them.

There is even a role that losers are supposed to play in the dressing room after an important game. Heads must be down, bodies slumped against lockers, no noise except for a lot of slamming about of equipment. Smashing clubhouse equipment is a good sign of "competitiveness." Any sign of happiness after a loss means that winning obviously isn't a very serious matter. There's not a book that says, "I'm a loser but I'm happy, and I enjoy what I'm doing." You seldom hear anyone say, "Well, we lost but we played the best we could. We really gave 'em hell and we can be proud of that." Instead, the idea is that you must suffer, especially after league play-offs and championship games. The team that finishes second is not allowed to look back on its season with any special joy; already it must be focused on what will be a "frustrating" off-season, and then "revenge" the following year. This denial of losing reflects a society in which there is little sympathy for the loser. "Losing is the great American sin," said the late John R. Tunis, a longtime critic of the American sports ethic. "There is such a thin line between winning and losing. Yet the laurels only go to the winner. The rush is always to the champion." Losers are the butt of our jokes—or the target of our scorn and frustrations. If most coaches and players seem neurotically obsessed with losing, we need only look into the stands to understand part of the reason. Former Chicago linebacker Dick Butkus described the extremists among football fans: "I was in New England the day they threw bottles at their own team. They think the $7 they pay for a ticket entitles them to do anything, but I think of them as $7 animals. People don't know what the players on a losing team go through. It's a tough business, and it is a business."

Another reason for the inability of those in sports to accept defeat is the realization that was expressed by former pro receiver Peter Gent in his novel *North Dallas Forty*: "Winning is a matter of opinion. But losing is a cold reality." Winning is always temporary, but losing is permanent. You win for just a short time but you lose forever; it always haunts you. Those who try to display equanimity in defeat are often taunted by remarks such as "Nice guys finish last" or "Show me a good loser and I'll show you a loser." In the eyes of most coaches, these athletes obviously lack the competitive drive, the "killer instinct." Said that kindly old competitor, Leo Durocher: "Show me a good loser in professional sports, and I'll show you an idiot. Show me a sportsman, and I'll show you a player I'm looking to trade." But nobody has plunged lower than ex-University of Minnesota basketball coach Bill Musselman, who posted this message over his team's shower entrance: "Defeat Is Worse Than Death Because You Have to Live with Defeat."

The incidents of mature responses when a team loses are rare. After the 1974 football season, when Green Bay head coach Dan Devine came under heavy criticism by his players, coaches, and Packer fans, quarterback Jim Del Gaizo rose to his defense. Del Gaizo argued that the problems stemmed from "too many thin-skinned players" failing to own up to their own shortcomings rather than from Devine. "When you lose, you start looking for somebody else to blame," Del Gaizo admitted. "If the guys want to blame the coaches, they can, but I can't blame anyone but myself. I know I played like a dog and I'm sure a lot of others didn't play up to their capabilities."

When his Seattle team lost eight out of ten games early in his first season as head coach, Bill Russell responded: "If we lose every game the rest of the season, the world will go right on. I'll go right on living—I enjoy life, every phase of it." Unfortunately, every Russell is countered by a hundred George Allens. Allen once wrote, "Life without victory is tasteless. It is possible for a loser to drive a big car, but it is not possible for him to enjoy it." Allen's college counterpart, Woody Hayes, has said: "Anyone who tells me, 'Don't worry that you lost, you played a good game anyway,' I just hate." Rhetoric like this from men who are in the limelight simply reinforces the losing mystique. Even a coach like Penn State's Joe Paterno, who today is seen as a heretic by many of his colleagues because he doesn't share their conviction that victory is everything in life, had to overcome his "losing" phobia. His wife told *Sports Illustrated* writer William Johnson that he couldn't handle losing in his early years as a coach. "He'd shut the door and not come out," she said. "He was a real s.o.b." After his first Penn State team in 1966 finished 5–5, Paterno was "despondent." His wife continued: "He said that if he didn't have a winning season the second year he would quit and go back to assistant coaching. He said it wasn't fair to the kids to be coached by a loser."

This pervasive abhorrence of losing is, in fact, part and parcel of a coarse American phenomenon: we simply do not accept losing, whether it's in Vietnam or in international competitions such as the Olympics. We're inculcated almost from birth that "Americans are winners" in everything we do. As Paterno has said:

I think our whole country has been twisted a little bit because we don't know how to lose. This was basically our problem in Vietnam. Nobody had the courage to tell the American people, "Look, we got licked. Let's get out." Because we weren't mature enough to do this, we lost many young lives that we needn't have lost.

In a *Sports Illustrated* article after the 1972 Munich Olympics, Bil Gilbert discussed American attitudes towards international sports competition:

When we have won, we have crowed that the victories display the superiority of representative democracy, free enterprise and grants-in-aid over other ways of doing things. This behavior has done much to promote an Ugly American image and convince men and women the world over that one of the true pleasures available today is beating an American at some game. When we have lost, we have invariably whined that we were beaten because the other side injected politics into the contest and cheated by putting its system to work producing winning athletes.

There have been two glaring examples in recent years of American petulance in defeat. The first was our upset loss to Russia in the basketball finals at Munich, the first time we had ever lost in Olympic competition. The Russians had showed very clearly the American ideal: If you work long enough and hard enough, you're going to win eventually. But we couldn't handle it. Controversial and unfair as our loss was, the immature behavior on the part of our players, coaches, and Olympic officials was overwhelming. We pouted. We denied it. We even refused to show up to accept the second-place medals.

Even more blatant was our sour-grapes response to the extraordinary success of the Taiwan Little Leaguers when they won four consecutive Little World Series in Williamsport, Pennsylvania, between 1971 and 1974. In 1973, instead of applauding Taiwan's brilliant play, which emphasized perfection of textbook fundamentals, American spectators would boo when the Taiwanese took the field. Later, dismayed Little League officials dispatched a task force to Taiwan in a crude, unsuccessful attempt to uncover rumored violations of eligibility, district size, and practice time. Bitterness and jealousy on the part of the Americans was again on display in 1974, but the Taiwanese never lost their cool. "They psyche everyone out," complained an official of the New Haven, Connecticut, team. He claimed that the heavy atmosphere around Williamsport caused the New Haven players to enter the game thinking a victory would save America from the Chinese.

All this childish behavior by adults led one girl to write to the *Los Angeles Times*: "Why is it so difficult for America to admit someone else is better at something—anything? I am proud of America but I'd be much prouder if Little League officials would salute Taiwan, a small but proud country, for the great players it turns out."

The Americans, of course, finally got even by taking their balls and bats and going home. In late 1974, Little League Baseball Inc. simply decreed that foreign teams no longer would be permitted to compete at Williamsport, reasoning that the World Series was "out of proportion," and that it was "developing trends that are out of control." President Peter McGovern said the decision was based on studies which showed that youngsters under 12 "should not be subjected to the pressure of the game," meaning a World Series. Of course, critics of the Little League had long contended that such was the case, only to be rebuffed until the argument served as a useful scapegoat for those in control. In that same vein, one Little League official admitted that the American *players* weren't annoyed at the domination of the Taiwan teams. "The kids raised no objections. If it was up to the kids, Taiwan would still be in." But as usual, the decision was made by the adults.

Immature Behavior

I've been led to believe that in a competitive society, the ultimate is to feel worthwhile, to feel contented, to feel you've accomplished something. But as we've seen in this chapter, there seems to be far too little self-satisfaction in professional sports today. We have adults playing children's games for high stakes while perpetuating the children's behavior. Tommy Prothro admitted as much when he became the Los Angeles Rams head coach several years ago: "I think everybody in athletics is immature. They're always seeking something. . . . When I say immature, I say it by the standards set up by sociologists, psychologists, and psychiatrists. Their ideals are peace, contentment, and relaxation. People in sports aren't seeking that. Their focus is competitiveness." What Prothro seems to be saying is that people in sports are seeking misery, anxiety, and tension, and that these qualities are somehow related to competitiveness. You have to be a little crazy to want to feel like that. And yet an article by Vince Lombardi in the *Saturday Evening Post* was entitled "Pro Football Is for Madmen." Strange how we remember his quote "Winning isn't everything. It's the only thing," but not "Pro football is for madmen."

One result of the special blending of pressure, money, and hothouse nurturing of superstars is the immature behavior that often emerges. Chicago columnist Mike Royko suggests that the term *superjerks* might be an appropriate label for those athletes who say and do such remarkable things that the word *jerk* doesn't do them justice. He defines the superjerk as "the superstar who won't simply kick, hit, throw, or maim something, and call it a day. The superjerk is not content with earning large sums of money while getting wholesome exercise. He must constantly display his superego, indulge in superwhining, superbragging, superspending and superpouting."

Another perspective was offered by former playing great Bill Russell after his first year as coach of the Seattle Supersonics: "I have this marvelous club up in Seattle. We have the young millionaires. Everybody has a no-cut contract, and they have clauses in their contracts that say no cut, no hassle, don't bug me, and I'll play when I feel like it. I went there from another century. I was still a gladiator. You fight for the job and take pride in what you do."

The young millionaires who strap on their skates in hockey have been termed "spoiled brats posing as professionals" by critic Stan Fischler, who added, "They are constantly complaining, always ready to lay the blame on the coach, always ready to sulk and pack their bags." Detroit columnist Joe Falls feels that hockey players are "getting to be as strange a bunch of birds as we have in pro sports. They're just as spoiled as so many of our other athletes." He cited the case of Marcel Dionne, who was then with the Red Wings:

He is a talented young player and basically a fine young man. But he has been spoiled. He has known little discipline. Ever since his junior playing days, people have been giving him things, taking him places and fawning over him as if he were a Hollywood idol. All that Dionne has known is adulation. He has never known a hungry day as a hockey player. He has always had money in his pocket.

One of the strange beliefs that underlie the notion of competition is the assumption that if a person is competitive, he also possesses other positive characteristics. The athlete can throw a racket, start fights, use "gamesmanship" to distract and disrupt his opponent, throw tantrums, deliberately roughhouse another player, or curse the officials, and it's dismissed because "He's a hell of a competitor. He wants to win." The athlete can be immature or childish or destructive, but because he "wants to win," this excuses his behavior. We surely wouldn't give the same consideration to a bank robber who beat up a teller and three customers, if his lawyer's defense was, "He's a hell of a competitor. He really wanted to rob that bank. He's the number three ranked bank robber in Colorado."

I talked earlier about Jimmy Connors' meteoric rise to the top of the tennis world. Hand in hand with his brilliant talent went, unfortunately, the kind of courtside tactics and manners that would have been judged aberrant behavior fifteen years ago. He would berate officials, put down linesmen when they made calls he felt were in error, insult his opponents, give heckling fans obscene gestures, dawdle when he was behind, and in general violate the standards of sportsmanship that have been an important element in the game's style. His arrogance was justified, of course, under the guise of his being highly competitive and driven (just as millions of Americans over-looked Bobby Fisher's rude, petulant, boorish behavior simply because he beat the Russian in their chess showdown in 1972). Sure enough, at Forest Hills a year later, television commentator Tony Trabert said of Connors: "He's a very gifted competitor. He wants to win in the worst way."

"People don't seem to understand that it's a damn war out there," said Connors. "Maybe my methods aren't socially acceptable to some, but it's what I have to do to survive. I don't go out there to love my enemy, I go out there to squash him." In other words, the means justify the end, as long as they lead to winning. But my feeling is that if this is what it's going to take to reach the top in tennis, then we can expect that behavior to become the model. Connors's approach will become the path to success. But what will we do one day when the best twenty-five players in the field exhibit that behavior? Tennis will be a zoo. And then a player will come along who is superdisciplined and a perfect gentleman and he'll win everything, and then the reaction will be, "You've got to learn to be disciplined."

Alistair Cooke, the British historian and newsman, summed it up very neatly, in discussing sports in America: "This is the age of the prima donna. . . . The crowd loves a character. . . . [But] what we're doing today is subsidizing bad behavior. The whole theory of sports has changed. The word itself has gone by the board. Sport and sportsmanship have the same root, but sportsmen are a disappearing species."

3

Sports Don't Build Character— They Build Characters

PERHAPS THE MOST enduring rationale for partici- pating in athletics is the belief that sports build character. As far back as the 1920s, this myth that competition leads to desirable personality traits was in the national consciousness. John R. Tunis, a sportswriter who was forty years ahead of most of his cohorts in questioning the intrinsic value of sports, wrote:

The Great Sports Myth . . . is a fiction sustained and built up by . . . the news-gatherers [and other] professional sports uplifters . . . who tell us that competitive sport is health-giving, character-building, brain-making, and so forth. . . . They imply more or less directly that its exponents are heroes, possessed of none but the highest of moral qualities; tempered and steeled in the great white heat of competition; purified and made holy by their devotion to . . . sport. Thanks to [coaches and sportswriters], there has grown up in the public mind an exaggerated and sentimental notion of the moral value of great, competitive sport spectacles. . . . Why not stop talking about the noble purposes which sports fulfill and take them for what they are? . . . In short let us cease the elevation of [sport] to the level of a religion.

The years since Tunis, in fact, have produced little documentation to support the character-building theory of sports. In his book *Sociology of Sport*, Dr. Harry Edwards compiled a list of characteristics that are ascribed to athletic participation: character development, loyalty, altruism, discipline, fortitude, preparation for life, opportunities for advancement, physical fitness, mental alertness, educational achievement, religiosity, and nationalism. Based on exhaustive research, Edwards found that in all cases the evidence for such claims was inconclusive, unsubstantiated, or nonexistent. "The claims made on behalf of sport do not have a sufficient basis in current knowledge to justify the dogmatic certainty with which they are expressed," he concluded.

The evidence appears to be that the athlete who reaches the top (or who fails) would have done so despite his surface personality traits. In 1971, Dr. Bruce Ogilvie and I wrote in *Psychology Today*: "For the past eight years we have been studying the effects of competition on personality. Our research began with the counseling of problem athletes, but it soon expanded to include athletes from every sport, at every level from the high school gym to the professional arena. On the evidence gathered in this study . . . we found no empirical support for the tradition that sport builds character. Indeed, there is evidence that athletic competition limits growth in some areas. It seems that the personality of the ideal athlete is not the result of any molding process, but comes out of the ruthless selection process that occurs at all levels of sport. Athletic competition has no more beneficial effects than intense endeavor in any other field. . . . Sport is like most other activities—those who survive tend to have stronger personalities."

One athlete who feels that sports is failing to build "sound minds in sound bodies" is George Sauer, the former All-Pro receiver for the New York Jets. Sauer has said:

It's interesting to go back and listen to the people on the high school level talk about sport programs and how they develop a kid's self-discipline and responsibility. I think the giveaway that most of this stuff being preached on the lower level is a lie is that when you get to the college and professional levels, the coaches still treat you as an adolescent. They know damn well that you were never given a chance to become responsible or self-disciplined. Even in the pros you are told when to go to bed, when to turn your lights off, when to wake up, when to eat, and what to eat. You even have to live and eat together like you were in a boys' camp.

Another skeptical athlete is former San Francisco quarterback John Brodie, who was quoted in *Psychology Today* as saying, "Sport is one of the few activities in which many Americans spend a great deal of time developing their potentialities. It influences character, I think, as much as our schools and churches do. But, even so, it falls far below what it could be. It leaves out so much. I would love to see a sports team developed with a more fulfilling purpose." In Brodie's view, "sport is so important in creating values in America" that it should be "more than winning at any cost, more than beating people up and making money and getting ahead over somebody else's dead body."

While some personality traits do become modified and developed as a result of the social experiences and pressures inherent in competitive athletics, all too often we endow our athletes with virtues that have nothing to do with how fast they run or how well they shoot the ball. The "halo effect" often protects the athlete from a censure he may deserve and helps to provide him with attributes he may not necessarily possess. For instance, many fans assume that a person in sports who wins and reaches the top has all the desirable traits. He is, in fact, given credit for having traits that have nothing to do with winning. He is seen as a nice guy, modest, sincere, and considerate of others. Conversely, the loser is often judged by the fan to be weak and lacking in character.

Basketball great Bill Russell, a man of refreshing candor,

once said: "This business about an athlete being so great is a fiction. It is a fiction written by nonathletes who may be acting out their own fantasies. One who writes about athletes sometimes gets to admire them so much, he doesn't accept the real person; or if he sees flaws in his hero, he ignores them." It has been a great shock for some people in recent years to find that their sports heroes are really human and that they have a great many undesirable traits. Witness the hostile reaction by many disillusioned football fans during the 1974 strike, as they listened to the vitriolic language and self-serving arguments that passed back and forth between players and owners.

After observing months of what he termed "nasty behavior, distasteful words and disgusting actions on both sides," San Francisco columnist Wells Twombly concluded: "This is tribal warfare, pure and brutal. . . . It all speaks so well of character building and all that. If a single boy-child in this nation actually feels uplifted by all this, then somebody ought to get his name. The reaction has been quite the opposite."

Where did we get the notion that sports makes such an important contribution to man and mankind? First, we have testimonies by famous people who tie their success to previous athletic participation. Second, we hear from those within the profession who seek to justify what they're doing. And third, we have national leaders and banquet speakers telling us so. A few examples will illustrate the point.

Gen. Douglas MacArthur: "[Sport] is a vital character builder. It molds the youth of our country for their roles as custodians of the republic. It teaches them to be strong enough to know they are weak, and brave enough to face themselves when they are afraid. It teaches them to be proud and unbending in honest defeat, but humble and gentle in victory. . . . It gives them a predominance of courage over timidity, of appetite for adventure over loss of ease. Fathers and mothers who would make their sons into men should have them participate in [sports]."

Jess Hill, then the athletic director of the University of Southern California: "Athletics develop a dedication and a desire to excel in competition, a realization that success requires hard work and that life must be lived according to rules. A youngster can learn a sense of loyalty and a respect for discipline, both of which are lacking in this country today. . . ."

Sociologist David Riesman: "The road to the board room leads through the locker room."

The Little League motto: "From the ranks of boys who stand now on the morning side of the hill will come the leaders, the future strength and character of the nation."

Gerald Ford: "Broadly speaking, outside of a national character and an educated society, there are few things more important to a country's growth and well-being than competitive athletics. If it is a cliché to say athletics build character as well as muscle, then I subscribe to the cliché."

Those who believe in all-out competition and the verities of sports will invariably point to some glaring success story, such as Supreme Court Justice Byron "Whizzer" White, the former football All-American, or President Ford himself, a standout for Michigan in the early 1930s. The message is, "See what football did for these men." Yet to attribute their ultimate success to sports is misleading. They had successful personality styles to begin with, and sports just happened to be one of the things they took up; even if they hadn't participated, they would have been a success in other fields.

Similarly, every season we read about the youngster who fought his way out of the ghetto by playing basketball, or the truck driver's son who signed a football contract for $250,000. Thousands of other examples abound where sports have helped give a sense of direction to youngsters who lacked ambition or direction or responsibility, or who stuck it out in high school simply because they wanted to be on the football team.

This is fine. But what I object to is having these examples brought out to supposedly justify all the youngsters who are damaged by sports, physically or psychologically. We have verification only by highly successful people. We don't have failures say, "Look, I also didn't make it when I was playing football. I just sat on the bench and caused a lot of trouble." Nor do we have people suggesting that sports may be instrumental in destroying character. We never seem to hear the story of Fenwick, a nice kid who got along with his friends, had good grades, and liked his parents. Then he went out for high school football. As a result, he had three teeth knocked out, he dislocated his shoulder, he was too tired after practice to study and his grades fell apart, he hated his coach, and one day he took a tire iron to a kid he didn't like.

I had a friend whose son had just finished his second year of Little League. The boy had bad marks in school and problems with deportment, but he was a great Little League ball player. He was even named the team's most valuable player. However, two weeks later he was picked up for stealing. What moral fiber was sports helping to build in this youngster? They took Little League away, and he didn't have anything.

It could even be argued that many of President Nixon's problems could be traced back to his old football days as a bench warmer at Whittier College. Nixon told a pro football Hall of Fame gathering in 1971: "Chief Newman, my coach, an American Indian, produced some very fine teams at that small, little college at Whittier. . . . There were no excuses for failure. He didn't feel sorry for you when you got knocked down."

Writer Robert Lipsyte later noted in the *New York Times Magazine*: "Sports is a human process shaped by a society, and Nixon was nourished by the specific values of sport—team loyalty, discipline, perseverance, physical courage, respectful fear and hatred of the opposition, winning as the only criterion for success."

When we talk about "building character," my criteria are not that an athlete receive a college scholarship, sign a pro contract, and make a lot of money. The goal of those in sports should be to develop more mature, contented people who are emotionally and physically healthy.

We should all admire the coach who is trying to achieve this in his players, the coach who can say, "Harvey's become a hard worker and he's getting better grades now" because of his involvement in sports. I would respect any coach—regardless of his won-lost record—who told me, "Okay, if you don't believe me, here's what I've done. For the last ten years, I've kept track of each one of my players. They all have a job today, they've been promoted, they're active in community work, they're good family men, and they're happy." Tennessee basketball coach Ray Mears has made an effort to do this, and he has one of the most successful records in college history. He's clearly concerned about his players and he follows their progress after they graduate. It is also important that a coach keep track of all of his athletes, not just the successful ones. If he takes credit for the successes, he should also take responsibility for the failures.

I think one only has to look at reality—if you will, the daily sports page—to realize that while sports may indeed be building character in certain athletes, it is also building characters. The way the sports establishment handles these "characters" is an example of the fallacy that athletic competition automatically produces a "good" person. Deviant personalities—"troublemakers"—are screened out at every stage of the way through youth, scholastic, and collegiate sports. Those who do survive into the pros certainly don't receive sensitive handling. If the player is a questioning, doubting, independent, and outspoken soul, he's usually branded as a bad egg, an unfortunate draft choice, or a trade that went sour. Unless this athlete has a bright, perceptive, patient coach, he'll be cut or traded or allowed to waste away his talent by feuding with those who say he has a "bad attitude." Instead of trying to help the athlete work out his problem, instead of trying to act in a humanistic fashion, the club says, "Trade him, we don't need that kind of trouble." Which is a lousy way to run a franchise that might be worth $15 million.

If sports were really building character, most of these athletes would be able to resolve their problems. I do not mean to imply, however, that the problems are *all* with the coaches or owners. There are athletes who have deep-seated problems and who will continue to make trouble wherever they go. Athletics should be an area where these problems are more easily detected; what is even more important, it should be an area where there is at least a start in helping athletes with their problems.

4

The Destructive Pro Model

AT THIS POINT, parents or coaches might argue, "Look, you're talking about professional sports—but the pros have nothing to do with us." I strongly disagree. In my opinion, the professionals (and many of their collegiate counterparts) are becoming an increasingly destructive model for childhood sports, from coaching styles to the competitive ethos, and if left unchecked, this madness will eventually undermine the inherent values of organized sports.

First, there is the win-at-all-costs lunacy, which sets the competitive tenor for many of the adults who run our childhood sports programs. We have already seen how this obsession with success can be rationalized at the professional level, where the coach has to win to save his job and the athlete has to be a winner to hold his position on the team. Unfortunately, the philosophy is now contaminating play at the Pop Warner-Little League level, where the idea should be to learn the sport, have fun, and not be consumed by the pressures and emotions that go hand in hand with an emphasis on winning.

The continuous exposure to the professionals in all sports, all year round, in all the media constantly reminds us that the only reason for participating is to win. The usual argument is, "If you don't play to win, why play at all?" Many people, in fact, tend to believe that winning-at-all-costs must go hand in hand with competition. But there is a clear difference between the two. To learn to compete and face a challenge, to learn to accept victory and adjust to defeat, is quite different from a philosophy whereby one individual or team must emerge as a victor. The benefits of competition are clearly abused when the final score is the only criterion. For example, a true competitor can find a great deal of personal pride in having played his best even when he loses. But many of us have the erroneous belief that if you play your best you will win, so if you don't win, you feel frustrated and cheated. It takes more courage to admit you played your best and lost than to say you played poorly and won.

Secondly, though many pro athletes want to deny it, they are important models for children. If the pros exhibit immature, selfish, destructive, or exhibitionistic behavior, they can expect young athletes to do the same thing. One has only to watch a youth hockey game, where the players raise their sticks after a goal, or youth football, where youngsters "spike" the ball in the end zone after a touchdown, to see miniature professionals at work. Of course these are harmless mannerisms. At the same time, however, these children are absorbing the hostility and violence that is constantly on display, in person or on television. Further embellishment is added in newspapers and magazines when athletes defend the "intrinsic value" of aggression in their sport; that fighting, for instance, is a gallant act of manliness. This is hard enough to swallow objectively, let alone when your ten-year-old hockey player comes home with a broken nose inflicted by a quick-tempered defenseman. When youngsters see the notoriety that comes to a Derek Sanderson or Philadelphia's Dave Shultz—the game's leading practitioner of on-ice violence—and when these players are not only tolerated but made into celebrities, is it any wonder that they are emulated?

Thirdly, many adults and coaches believe that professional sports serve as healthy, inspirational goals for young athletes. "Isn't this what we're working towards?" they ask. I'm all in favor of people seeking to excel in a sport and trying to reach the top, *if* that is their choice—not one imposed by a parent or coach—and they are fully aware of the vast disparity between the millions who start out with high hopes and the mere thousands who actually succeed. What I strongly oppose, however, is having the professional athlete used as a living model of a way of life. There is very little evidence that sports and competition lead to happiness, beauty, love, or even a productive life. In fact, as the previous chapters have pointed out, the well-scrubbed Jack Armstrong image is being steadily corroded by the destructive model of professional sports. I read the sports pages and watch televised games and I think, "This is the model for our kids? Do we think *this* is developing character?"

What we have to do is take the pro athlete off his pedestal. He isn't a hero; he's a man (or woman) with a physical capacity to excel at a sport. He is basically selfish—meaning his first thought is usually for himself—and we have deliberately bred him to entertain us by playing games. As basketball great Bill Russell said, "I've never seen an athlete, including myself, who I think should be lionized. There are very few athletes I know whom I would want my kids to be like. The only kids I try to set an example for are mine." Mike Marshall, the Los Angeles relief pitcher, once refused autographs to a group of youngsters, explaining that he would willingly sign if the boys could show him that their autograph books also contained the signatures of their teachers and others who were really meaningful in their lives.

A similar plea was made by Joe Paterno, the highly successful football coach who turned down a million-dollar offer from the New England Patriots in order to stay at Penn State. "What the hell's the matter with a society that offers a *football coach* a million dollars?" he asked *Sports Illustrated* writer William Johnson. "I get letters from people who seem to think that if only Joe Paterno can spend 20 minutes with a kid then his troubles will be over. Nuts! People want to give me too much credit. I'm a football coach who has won a few games—remember? Now what the hell does *that* mean? If I were an accountant no one would pay that much attention to me, right?"

San Francisco columnist Wells Twombly presented a viewpoint in 1972 that is just as relevant today:

Anybody who has lived through the incomparable greed of the past ten years and still thinks that sweating in public still has its uplifting aspects needs ten hours with a good shrink. Not only is it obvious that sports do not build character, it is even questionable if they have any socially redeeming aspects.

Do small boys honestly still look up to athletes? If so, they are getting one hell of a gruesome lesson in just how graspy human beings can be. In a sense, maybe that's better for them. At least they won't grow up with any false impressions about the nobility of man.

Despite the pleas for sanity and for a badly needed perspective on what has become a nationwide mania, our infatuation with the pros continues to thrive. Young lives everywhere get channeled in the direction of a sports career. After all, where else can a person who "makes it" find a job that can match professional sports in a short work year, big money, good pension plan, notoriety, social benefits, and establishment of contacts for the day when the knee goes out or retirement comes? To further enhance the image of a pro athlete in the eyes of his public, there is a curious phenomenon at work: the longer he plays the more recognition he gets, and the more recognition he gets the more money he makes, and the more money he makes the more he acquires the "halo effect," until finally we have a "day" for him. He's making more money than the general manager and head coach combined, not to mention 95 percent of those in the stands, but we give him a couple of new cars, furniture, clothes, tickets to Hawaii, and a gold-plated jockstrap to show our appreciation. But just what has this athlete contributed to society during that period of time? He has been an entertainer—for some of us, some of the time—but little more.

Defenders of the pro athlete will argue, "Look at the contribution these people are making—the charities they help support, the youth groups they help in the off-season, the inspiration they give when they visit children's hospitals." My feeling is that if someone does it voluntarily, without notoriety, without financial reimbursement, then they are to be commended. We need to recognize those athletes who are in fact helping society and their sport by contributing their money or their time to the things they are concerned about, such as giving free coaching clinics at urban recreation centers. But all too often, athletes simply lend their name or make an appearance—for a fee, of course. (Athletes are not always to blame for this state of affairs. Our vision of professional sports is so warped and battered that we are instantly suspicious of the athlete with the clean-cut image. For example, a top player will come along who does everything right: he willingly signs autographs, he visits children in the hospital, he pays his taxes and tips the mailman at Christmas, he maintains his dignity whether he wins or loses, and he never stirs up controversy. Baffled by this behavior, sportswriters set the poor guy up for the kill by dubbing him "colorless" or "old-fashioned" or "image-conscious," and the public begins to wonder, "What's wrong with this guy? What is he after?" Not until he beats up a teammate can we relax a little.)

John Wooden once said, "Every person in the public eye has a deep moral responsibility to youth and to the public." An extreme, but very tragic, example of what he meant was Evel

Knievel and his aborted jump over the Snake River Canyon in 1974. Millions of Americans saw Knievel as an heroic figure, someone who represented the individualistic spirit of the nation. Granted he is a somewhat charismatic figure, if one could stomach the blatant commercialization and gladiator overtones of his venture, but the ultimate tragedy was those youngsters (and adults) who were subsequently injured or even killed as a result of emulating his jump, over dry creek beds and the like. In denying any guilt or responsibility for these victims, Knievel and his supporters failed to realize that children did not have the benefit of professional consultation and million-dollar equipment. These youngsters only saw Knievel's fame and fortune; he was "doing his thing," and they simply wanted to be like him.

If the professionals continue to be the most important model for childhood sports, it will eventually destroy sports as we know them. The pro influence, rather than serving as a virtuous model, will squeeze out the simple joys and satisfactions of playing a game with friends while substituting the dog-eat-dog ethics of the rest of society. Veteran basketball player Bill Bridges, who enjoyed All-Pro status and played on an NBA championship team, offered this perspective:

Based on what I've seen and received from pro basketball—and despite how I feel about the people in it—I'd go into something else if I could start over again. Basketball has instilled certain beneficial things in me. They'll come out after I leave the sport, I hope, and I'll make mature growth in another field. But I'd prefer it if my son thought of athletics as being completely for recreational purposes.

Fortunately there are a growing number of parents, coaches, and sports programmers who share these sentiments, who want to steer clear of the pro model, except when it comes to teaching youngsters the correct techniques. These adults want to involve youngsters in competitive sports in a healthful, supportive, humanistic way, so that they will be encouraged to remain physically active the rest of their lives.

These and other areas of concern—especially the emotional, psychological, and interpersonal aspects of competitive sports for children—will serve as the focus for the remainder of this book. We have seen the total picture of what is happening in American sports today. With that as a backdrop, we can now concentrate on the childhood level, starting in the next chapter with the need for parents to evaluate the influences that led to their child's participation in sports.

5

The Myths of
Early Competition

Charlie Brown, talking to Linus in the *Peanuts* comic strip:
"Life is just too much for me. I've been confused from the day I
was born. I think the whole trouble is that we're thrown into
life too fast. We're not really prepared."

Linus: "What did you want . . . a chance to warm up first?"

IF LEFT TO THEIR OWN DEVICES, most youngsters
take up a sport just to be with their friends and to have fun.
They don't start out putting the emphasis on winning that
their parents and coaches do. Their greatest achievement, in
fact, is simply to belong, to be a member of a team or a club.
The second biggest thing in their life is to make a contribution—to play, not to sit on the bench. Belonging and
contributing are normal needs, which can be fulfilled by all of
us. But they are being subverted at the childhood level by a
gilt-edged emphasis on winning and competition.

I feel that competition is a learned phenomenon, that people
are not *born* with a motivation to win or to be competitive. We
inherit a potential for a degree of activity, and we all have the
instinct to survive. But the will to win comes through training
and the influences of one's family and environment. As the
song in *South Pacific* says, "you've got to be carefully taught."
The song is talking about prejudice, but it's the same thing.

From a very early age we are bombarded by direct, indirect, subtle, behavioral, and verbal messages to the effect that the important thing in life is to be a winner—and the earlier the better. If you want to be a successful high school athlete you must specialize, and specialize early.

In view of these influences, parents should question their own particular attitude towards athletics. Some parents, for instance, believe that the most important reason for sports participation is to have youngsters learn to compete. When the father vows, "My boy is going to learn to become a competitor!" his assumption is that the child will learn to set goals, to test his limits, to acquire more self-discipline, and to deal with the emotional ups and downs that are a reflection of real life. But as we have seen, the idea that sports help build a competitor is a common misperception. Sports may, in fact, be burning the competitive spirit and turning youngsters off athletics. Dr. Muzafer Sherif, a social psychologist at Penn State, points out in *The Physician and Sportsmedicine* that even though competition is normal doesn't mean it's healthy and in the best interest of the child. "We cannot assume that just because the child is competing it's a good catharsis, a healthy release," he says. "It can lead to hostility or good sportsmanship, the results depending on how the competition is organized." He favors a situation where the competition is set up in a cooperative way, as opposed to having winning as the all-important goal.

Other parents strongly believe that "winning is the name of the game," without actually stopping to think what winning really means. For instance, a Queens, New York, Little League official argues, "This is not an instructional league. We're here to win. There's nothing wrong with winning." But why can't the two—instruction and winning—coexist? A win-or-else attitude overlooks the large number of sports-loving youngsters who are weeded out along the way because they lack talent; the youngsters who must ride the bench ("This is a big game—we can't afford to lose"); the players who are made to feel miserable because they lost or contributed directly to a defeat; and the small number of winners there really are in sports. The problem, I think, is that many parents don't know any measurement for success except "Who won?"

It's interesting to note that children often have a different perspective of what sports are about. When they play tennis, for example, and adults aren't around to ask "Who's winning?" the idea is to keep the ball going back and forth, even if it bounces two or three times or goes off the court. That's the thrill; not to slam the ball down the opponent's throat. Unfortunately, the adults soon come along and start insisting that the youngsters "play by the rules"; that is, play to win.

"How can they have fun," we reason, "if they don't play to win? If there's not a situation created where one side wins and the other loses?" At a Little League meeting one night, an obviously uptight father interpreted what I was saying as "Let's not have the kids compete." Was that my philosophy? Because his feeling was that "Competition is life."

I agreed that learning to compete obviously has merit, since one finds himself competing most of his life, either with others or within himself. But I pointed out that adults share a common misconception: that children will not compete unless adults are around to take over and show them how. But children are competing all the time—in school, at home, among their friends, on the playground. Given free time, they love to get into some kind of activity; they do it naturally. If a group of adults were to take eighteen youngsters who liked to play baseball out on the field, and were to hang around just to answer questions about technique, the youngsters would soon choose up teams and they sure as hell would compete. They would work out a balance in the teams and adjust to any imbalance naturally. They wouldn't have uniforms and nobody would be keeping statistics, but everybody would play the entire game and they would all have fun. What's equally important, it would be a growth experience; they would be doing it themselves rather than having the adults run the show.

I realize those days are past, except in small towns and on inner-city streets and playgrounds, when youngsters would organize their own games on dusty sandlots, rock-strewn fields, and frozen ponds. Much as I lament the passing of the old tradition, I know that such a system is impractical if one of our purposes is—and should be—to open up sports to as many children as possible, no matter what their skill or native ability. We need parents and other interested adults to be involved in youth leagues in order to help things run smoothly, and to offer technical advice so that youngsters will improve their skills. The problem is that adults feel they have to organize and run *everything*, from determining the starting line-ups to calling the plays in football, and eventually they can strangle much of the fun by imposing all their rules, traditions, and grandstand pressures. Instead, when the game begins they should think about withdrawing as coaches and overzealous spectators and let the kids learn to run their own affairs, with their own self-imposed pressure to play well.

As I said earlier, I'm not against competition. Everybody *likes* to win. But there's a vast difference between competing for the fun of competing, and regimenting everything with only one goal in mind—to produce a league champion.

Most children in this country, when they reach the age of five or six, can generally find an organized sport waiting for them at the nearest playground, recreation center, gym, skating rink, or swimming pool. This American compulsion to organize everything for our young athletes reflects a growing belief by many parents that the earlier you learn a sport—the earlier you learn to *compete*—the better your chances are of becoming a professional or an Olympic hero. If, that is, you haven't been burned out, injured, or eliminated along the way. Once again we have applied an adult model to a growing child. We continue to raise our expectations of children while lowering the age at which they can compete. We fail to make the critical distinction between learning a sport in a fun, low-key situation and having to compete to win in that sport at a very early age. It's not *when* you start your child in sports that counts; it's what your goals are. If you are starting your five-year-old in ice hockey because you dream that he'll one day play for the Montreal Canadiens (even if you don't admit it to anybody), then your behavior is destructive. On the other hand, early involvement in sports can be a healthy outlet for the child who has sensitive, patient parents and coaches. Vermont ski coach Mickey Cochran, for example, put all four of his children on skis before they were four, not to develop champions but a love for the sport. As he explained:

Kids progress very rapidly when they learn that young. But at first you have to literally babysit for them. And be extremely patient. My wife and I made up our minds not to get angry or to criticize them for any reason, which took some real tongue-biting at times. We would just about have their skis on and they would say, "I have to go to the bathroom" or "I want a drink of water." All we wanted was for them to have fun. It should be that way with any kids in sports. It may be that they don't have a hankering to be Jean Claude Killy or a Henry Aaron.

Still, all four Cochrans made the U.S. ski team, and daughter Barbara Ann won the slalom gold medal at the 1972 Sapporo Olympics.

Vic Braden, the innovative tennis coach who is director of the Vic Braden Tennis College in Southern California, likes to start youngsters at age three or four. But he stresses that any coach who works with youngsters this young must analyze his motives:

If the coach is trying to develop champions, then he has to get out of the field because we don't need that approach. In tennis, his goals should be to introduce kids to a terrific hand-eye coordination game and let them have fun, get exercise, play in the sun. Let the kid hit thousands of balls. Let him laugh his guts out and run all over the court. He may only hit one out of five over the net but he'll think he's sensational. The problem comes when the parents start shouting, "You can do it, Johnny! . . . Oh, God, you missed it again."

If the coach is secure in his ability to teach tennis and has analyzed why he's starting youngsters so young, then there will be a positive relationship in teaching sports to infants, Braden feels. He is currently researching his contention that tennis develops "a particular kind of hand-eye coordination that will be related to reading readiness, and that reading is going to improve through sports." Braden believes that an early start in sports—on a low-key basis—is important for another reason:

Kids who start out young, in a non-pressure situation, usually remember how much fun a game like tennis was. They might lay off for a year or two, get wrapped up in something else, but they always remember how much fun they had, and eventually they want to come back. But youngsters who don't pick up a game like tennis until high school, for instance, are now looking around to see who's watching. They can't afford to lose face and if they can't play very well you hear them mumbling, "This is a stupid, sissy game." Many of them never play again until they're secure enough on the inside to come back and try. They only remember how much humiliation there was to the game.

Cochran, Braden, and other enlightened coaches maintain that the following guidelines should serve for those parents and coaches who are dealing with very young, beginning athletes: (1) keep it fun, for the child as well as the adults; (2) be agonizingly patient; (3) reward effort, not performance, unless the performance deserves it; and (4) remember that the aim is simply to introduce the child to a sport in a noncompetitive environment where he can learn the fundamentals without the pressure of executing them in front of a critical audience.

Fierce competition should be the last step in the development of young athletes. They should first learn the skills of the sport, the give-and-take of participation, the enjoyment of being active. Children are naturally inquisitive; they want to know how to play a game and how to improve. As they gain confidence they will seek out competition at their own level.

Alas, the reverse is true for many youngsters. They are thrown into competitive sports before they have sufficient confidence and a proper grasp of the fundamentals. Adults are so anxious to test the skills of young athletes, and so worried that children will grow bored with sports unless they "play for keeps," that they try to build the roof of the house before they have the foundation. They put Fenwick in a situation where he must learn to perform a skill under pressure before he is comfortable with the sport. He may still be overcoming his fears of getting hit by a baseball, making a head-on tackle, or falling on the ice at full speed, when suddenly he also has to win. His coach wants to win. His parents want to see their boy win. The child who just wants to learn how to pick up a ground ball and throw it correctly to first base is confounded by the fact that he has to throw out the runner and kill a rally. Not only that, he stands to be accused of not listening or not trying if he goofs up. If he continues to fail, he may be relegated to the bench.

Anyone who has ever taken up a sport knows the frustration—almost impossibility—of trying to pick up a skill while being under pressure to perform that skill. But we expect this of our children all the time. The average person might feel very differently if he himself were once thrust into a pressure situation while being evaluated by his peers and his superiors. For example, how would a mechanic feel if he were suddenly shown a totally new type of engine, given a box of tools, and told to repair the engine while a gallery consisting of his neighbors, friends, and opponents from a competing garage cheered or booed, depending on how he fared with the engine?

The assumption in childhood sports seems to be that if children don't learn to compete early, they're not going to be able to compete later in life. Defenders of this ethic argue that man is competing from the day he is born, and that the rewards in society—good grades, a good job, even finding the right mate—go to the competitor, the person who knows how to win. Where better to learn to compete than in the gym or on the athletic field? A clinching argument, these people feel, is that there is just as much pressure on a youngster when he is taking a math test as when he's up at bat. "What's the difference?" they ask.

My rebuttal is that the athletic pressures are far more severe. When a youngster fails the math test, he's all alone; the teacher may be the only one who knows his real score. Nobody really gives a damn about his test, except maybe his parents. And they don't say, "Boy, on question four, you really understood your math!" But place this youngster on the basketball court and let him miss two free throws with the score tied late in the game: he knows it, his opponents know it, his coach knows it, his teammates know it, and the spectators know it. The poor youngster has nowhere to turn for support.

What if we could take television cameras into Mrs. Magoo's kitchen and show the country how she fixed bacon and eggs? And have people hanging from the rafters staring at the eggs being fried? We would probably see a lot of burned bacon and broken eggs. Perhaps we could even organize a Neighborhood Breakfast League and announce that we were going to pick the number one mother on the block and that everybody was in competition. All the husbands and children would be spectators, and the results and standings would be posted on large scoreboards in all the supermarkets.

Competition like this would cause all sorts of women to fall apart. They certainly would have a different attitude concerning breakfast; in fact, most of them wouldn't even want to get out of bed in the morning. Their husbands would have to be Designated Cooks.

Instead of a situation like this, however, we have some poor little ten-year-old who comes to the plate with the bases loaded in the last inning. The bat's heavier than he is, he's afraid he'll get hurt by the ball, he doesn't even know if he'll hit it—he's just praying for a walk. Yet everybody is evaluating him. Not only that, we tell him this is for his own good; it is building character! No wonder he has a distorted perception of sports—and adults.

I strongly believe that when we force competition prior to the child's capability of handling the pressures involved—and without the proper support and encouragement—the long-term detriments will outweigh any supposed benefits. The years between eight and twelve are a vital identifying period, a time when children are trying to find themselves, in a psychological sense. They are trying to determine their capabilities and their limitations; they want to learn to deal with certain problems and to handle them effectively; they are in the process of trying to relate to other people and trying to discover their own worth, to be of value; it's a period of building confidence and taking on an attitude about themselves.

Children use play during this period as one way of growing up, of "trying out" life, on their own level, at their own pace, among their peers. Play is necessary for their development and should have a serious place in society. Instead, adults have taken over children's play, as if to say that unstructured, unorganized, sandlot games are no longer possible or important in today's society, especially in the suburbs and small cities. If we continue to plunge children too quickly into a grown-up world and cheat them out of the opportunity to prepare for life in a low-key, low-pressure fashion, we can expect a generation of adults to emerge who are totally alienated from competitive sports.

Gale E. Mikles, chairman of Michigan State University's athletic education department, is among those who feel that America is going overboard in the push for competitive sports, especially with six- and seven-year-olds. A former college wrestling coach, Mikles says, "The competitive spirit comes too soon now for most children to handle, tearing down basic values taught at home and destroying valuable young friendships. What organized sport really does with kids is to break down their own individuality and train them to fit into a system. It does not help to develop their own personality." Bill Harper, a philosophy professor and director of intramural sports at Emporia State, Kansas, contends that competitive sports thwart playfulness. "What do coaches from the Little League up say when they want to praise a player?" he asks. "They say he is a hard worker. Any time you have games in which the participants have less control than the organizers about how they play, who they play, when they play, then it is not really play. Kids get started in sports because they are playful, but they get caught in a system where they are playing for other rewards."

By imposing a competitive ethic fashioned by adults, we may be damaging the child's growing-up process. We interfere with a positive development by telling the child that he's not any good in a particular area and by placing great emphasis on that lack of ability. If he continues to be criticized, or rides the bench every season, or always plays on a losing team with a coach who stresses that winning is the most important thing, he may start to take on the identity of a loser—"Ah, I'm no good." If children can't learn to enjoy themselves outside the confines of winning, if they are led to believe they are failures if they don't succeed, then what values are sports imparting?

Let's take the example of a youngster participating in Little League. He's led to believe that this artificially induced area has some value in the real world, perhaps that it is even a very vital part of life. If he doesn't do particularly well or his team doesn't win or he has a difficult time learning the skills, he may develop a sense that he's a failure. If he continues to try his best in a sport but continues to lose—in an environment where the stress is on winning—he may even begin to feel rejected by his coaches and parents. They may try to hide their disappointment, but you don't fool too many children. This feeling of rejection may begin to interfere with other areas of life, such as social interaction and schoolwork. Instead of athletics helping him develop in other areas, they can actually destroy areas that might be more vital in later life.

By introducing competition too early, by having screening devices, by picking All-Star teams, by handing out trophies and keeping league standings, by emphasizing batting averages and touchdown passes—by many subtle means—we remind the young athlete of whether or not he's a "winner." The trouble with placing an overriding importance on league championships and trophies is that these are unrealistic goals for all but a handful of people. When you start giving out trophies, you differentiate children; unless you give everyone the same kind of trophy, you're telling the loser, "You're different from the winner." But children know who the better ball players are. They're aware of where they stand and how good they are in comparison with their peers. To give out trophies simply accentuates this difference. It makes the youngster who doesn't have talent feel even less capable, and it gives a distorted perspective to the youngster who gets the higher trophy—not to mention his parents, who can display it on the mantel as evidence that they are raising a hell of an athlete, and must therefore be a hell of a set of parents.

6

Influences on
Sports Participation

WHEN A CHILD SIGNS UP for Little League or joins a
swim club, his decision is a culmination of influences by his
parents, family, neighborhood, and friends. In fairness, therefore, the parents should try to examine these influences before
their child gets caught up in what can be a relatively vicious
"leisure" activity.

Perhaps the first step parents should take is to explore the
role that sports play in the family. In some families, athletics is
peripheral to schoolwork, school activities, television, and
hobbies. The parents have never been physically active and the
youngster feels little pressure or motivation to go into sports.
Other parents, however, like to encourage their children to
participate in sports because of the social and physical benefits
they feel can be gained. If that perspective is maintained, fine.
But too many parents view success in sports as the most
important contribution one can make to the family image; the
child is out there to make the parents look good. If the child's
athletic achievements fail to match the parents' dreams, then he

has let the family down; he hasn't done what is expected of him. Similarly, in an achieving, aspiring family, the most visible way a child can show the proper drive and motivation is to participate in athletics and be successful. The nonathletic son who is caught in this situation can't help but feel his parents' disappointment.

Parents should also question themselves about the child's decision to participate. Did the child have a choice? Or was he (or she) slowly guided towards that end? The parents may think, "We're not pushing our kid—he wants all this." But are they really sure? Was their youngster truly interested in the sport before he went out for it, or was he doing it to please his father, his mother, or his peer group?

In some families, father may have had the unfulfilled dream of becoming a professional athlete. He may have played in high school or college or even on a semipro level, and now he's working out his fantasies through the child. He's going to see that his child is given every "opportunity" possible in order to become a successful athlete. Buying the child a football on his first birthday, taking him to a ball game before he can understand it, putting him in hockey skates as soon as he learns to walk—all of these are clues that either mother or father or both had plans for the child to participate in athletics, as opposed to the child deciding, "I like sports and I like to play." It's one thing for the father who was active in sports to encourage the willing and talented child to follow in his footsteps, but quite another for him to push the child into sports and then drive the child to capture the glory that was once his or was always denied him.

Many parents will try to rationalize the early shove they give a youngster by pointing to his subsequent success or active involvement. One Chicago mother, whose sixteen-year-old boy was playing five hockey games a week on two different teams, said proudly: "Gary really goes for hockey. He's come a long way. We had to practically push him on the ice to get him interested."

Pressures to compete can also occur in large families, where younger children are expected to participate in sports simply because their brothers and sisters were athletes and did well. This role has been set for the younger child and it's simply assumed that he will fall in line, even though he may not have the talent. People within the family are saying, "Well, everybody else played Pop Warner; you should be playing Pop Warner, too." But objective people outside the family are thinking, "Why is that boy playing football? He's too frail." (I will discuss later how the untalented or disinterested child in an athletically oriented family is caught in a difficult, often painful situation. If he doesn't have sensitive, supportive parents, he can easily become alienated.)

Another stimulus for participation may be the fact that sports are an important form of recognition on the block. If the majority of families are caught up in age-group swimming, certain parents may feel ostracized if their child is not also swimming. Some parents may even feel coerced into having their child participate. If, for example, their son is big physically, he's simply *expected* to turn out for the football team. The parents may be embarrassed if he would prefer to play a noncontact sport like golf or tennis, or not to participate at all. In that case they may force him into sports in order to save face for the family. This is especially true in the South, as typified by the comments of Georgia Tech football coach Pepper Rogers: "Football is exciting in the South because this is such a masculine-oriented country. The kids are brought up to consider it an honor and a privilege to play football. In a Southern high school you have to play football to be accepted as a man. It's like fighting for your country."

This is why it is vital that parents question their own expectations in regard to their child's involvement in sports. If they expect him to make them proud, then the child can never really win. He will be evaluated by his results, not his effort or his participation, simply because poor performances will reflect badly on the family. If the child is successful, he may be rewarded and reinforced by his parents, but he must also expect to share the glory with them. Parents are perfectly justified in having a sense of pride whenever their child is successful—"That's my boy!" But by the same token, if he fumbles or makes a key error, the parents must be supportive and encouraging. If they are going to accept the credit whenever their child is successful, then they must be willing to accept the blame when things go wrong. Otherwise they should stay at home—away from the grandstands—and let their child play in peace.

The Child as the Motivator

Parents, of course, are not always the ones pushing sports participation. Many times the child is the one who insists; he (or she) has his own need to compete, to be active, to achieve something with his physical talent. Still, reaction by the parents—how they handle the situation—is equally important.

Parents often say to me, "Our boy really wants to play Pop Warner football, but we want him to wait until he's in junior high. He says all his friends are playing and he doesn't want to wait that long. Besides, he thinks 'flag' football is for sissies. He's a good athlete and he's driving us crazy because he wants to play."

My feeling is that not allowing the child to participate if he wants to is just as bad as forcing him to participate. In both cases parents are imposing their values on the child. The child should be allowed to express his opinions, and if he really wants to play football, and he's aware of what the sport requires, then he should be allowed to play. The parents may question his decision and they should voice their concern. But out of respect for the child, they should let him play. The boy should be encouraged, however, to examine all that is involved, not just the glamour and excitement. If he has a discussion with

the coach and possibly watches several practices, his expectations might change and he might reconsider before getting
involved.

Parent-child discussions such as these are vital, because the
parents can never assume why the child wants to play. Very
often it's not so much the love of the sport as the fact that his
friends are all out there. Thus the parents could actually be
keeping their child from socializing. Another example is the
shy, uncoordinated child who baffles his parents by announc-
ing that he wants to play ice hockey. Some parents will try to
joke away his fantasy. "How can you expect to play hockey,
Fenwick, when you can't even stand up walking through the
house?" Comments like that are cruel. Even if the child is
going to be a terrible player, there is some reason why he
wants to play. The reward may simply be to belong to a team
and to wear a uniform. Instead of belittling Fenwick's
coordination, his parents should help him sign up for a league
and assure him that they will drive him to practices and games.
They should help him learn the fundamentals of the game—
how to skate, how to hold his stick, even how to put on his
uniform—without being critical. If he doesn't do anything
right but he really tries hard, then they should support his
effort.

I once dealt with a mother whose nine-year-old boy had just
joined a Little League team and who was afraid it was going to
hurt him psychologically. He was extremely clumsy, he was
afraid of the ball, and he obviously wasn't going to play very
much—even his sisters made fun of him. But when I talked to
the boy, I learned that he wasn't looking at baseball from the
talent standpoint; he didn't care that he was the worst player
on the team. Instead, he was happy because he belonged to
something. His uniform gave him a sense of identity. He was
with his friends. Little League, in his eyes, had nothing to do
with active participation; he was happy just to sit on the bench.
I told his mother that she should encourage her son's
participation rather than projecting her own embarrassment;

that Little League was so important to him, to take it away would create sheer terror.

The key at every stage of sports participation—whether the child is talented or untalented, pushing or being pushed—is for the parents to be supportive, not negative; understanding, not insensitive; and open-minded, not obsessive in regard to the relative "virtues" of winning and success.

Girls Entering Sports

Many of the factors that lead boys into sports can also apply to girls. For example, if most of the young girls in the neighborhood are involved in gymnastics, the parents may feel that their daughter should be involved, too. They don't like to answer questions of the neighbors—"Why doesn't Pam give it a try?" The daughter herself may want to join simply because all of her friends are participating; they all head for the gymnastics club after school and she doesn't have anybody to play with around home.

When there is no boy in the family, or when parents wanted a boy but happened to have a girl, many of their dreams can still center on what they had hoped for—a rough and tumble little athlete. The girl, in effect, becomes the surrogate boy. At an early age especially, if she is pushed or encouraged rather strongly to participate in sports, she doesn't have the ability to differentiate and she simply goes along with what is expected of her.

Some girls fall into sports naturally if most of their little friends on the block are boys and they learn to run and throw "like a boy." Up until puberty, in fact, girls can compete on a relatively equal basis with boys in most sports. What boy hasn't grown up in a situation where a girl was the fastest kid on the block, or the fastest swimmer, or the best tennis player?

A further example of the push that can come from children is the daughter who wants to play a sport that her parents consider "unfeminine" or in the male's domain, such as Little

League baseball. Once again, the parents need to understand *why* the daughter wants to play. Her competitive instincts may be best met by aggressive, fast-moving sports like hockey, soccer, and basketball. Or she may want to compete as part of a team, rather than participate in individual sports, which until recent years have been the main outlet for girls—gymnastics, swimming, figure skating, skiing, tennis, golf, etc.

Ideally, now that the barriers—physical as well as psychological—toward widespread participation by girls in nearly every sport are finally coming down, parents should allow their daughters the freedom to participate as they choose. Billie Jean King expressed it perfectly when she testified before the Senate Subcommittee on Education: "If sports provide such valuable training in self-discipline and pursuit of excellence, why is it that such benefits are only extended to forty-nine percent of the population?" Another perspective is offered by Irene Shea, 31-year-old third baseman for the Raybestos Brakettes, the world champs of women's softball: "It's funny— a father would never think of telling his daughter to deliberately flunk a test in school, yet he'd try to discourage her from playing sports too seriously. People should never try to discourage you from something you're good at. If your body is something you can do things with on a sports field, then you should be allowed to."

A couple of other benefits should result from girls moving pell-mell into organized sports. For one thing, it should bring fathers and daughters closer together. "It's always Dad favoring the boys," said one Los Angeles high school baseball coach. "If my daughter had played baseball, I would have been closer to her." And perhaps, suggests Robert Peterson in the *New York Times Magazine*, unisex baseball "may bring a subtle shift in the attitudes of Little League leaders who see the game as the first test of machismo for boys."

Conflicts over Participation

Conflicts can erupt in the family when the parents disagree with one another, or with the child, over the child's pending involvement in sports. For instance, if one parent is pushing sports (normally the father) and the other is violently opposed, a power struggle can ensue. The domineering father will say, "Johnny's going to play football; he has to learn to be a man." But the mother becomes overprotective, perhaps trying to shield the child from dangers that don't really exist. The father wants the child to grow up too quickly while the mother wants to hang on too long. In many cases the father will win out, especially if he was once a good athlete; he feels he knows "what's best" for his son. If the mother is ignored, however, I think it's unfair not only to the mother but also to the child, because she often has a certain sensitivity and awareness not shared by the father.

Instead of polarizing, the parents need to meet halfway by sitting down *together with the child* and communicating their differences. The mother who is worried about Johnny getting hurt can be reassured that father will buy him the best possible protective equipment. And Johnny can promise that if he does get injured (especially at practice, when his parents aren't around), he won't try to hide it just to be "tough" or to stay in the lineup. Perhaps the parents can even talk Johnny into playing another sport, where the injury risk is lower; for example, soccer instead of football, or basketball in place of hockey.

If, however, the child is lukewarm about participating, while his parents are anxious that he play, or one parent is pushing and the other is neutral, then again there should be an honest, give-and-take discussion. Unfortunately, one of the gross injustices of child rearing is that parents invariably impose their value structure on youngsters without genuinely listening to what the child has to say. Children are automatically thought to be a vacuum—not so much in regard to native intelligence as in lacking experience, and thus never really thinking. But children are thinking and observing all the time. It's just that parents tend either to ignore what their children say or to reinterpret it to them so that they end up saying what the parents want to hear.

For example, a boy will tell his parents, "I'm not sure whether I want to play baseball or not." The parents want him to compete so badly that they reinterpret what he's saying to fit their own needs. "Well, we'll drive you to the game and we'll make sure you get to all the practices," they say. But that is not what the boy said. The parents are worried that he can't get to practice on time; the boy's concern is "I don't know if I even want to be there."

But the boy gets the message: "Don't you dare suggest that you're not going to participate."

Some parents will argue, "Are you telling me that I should always listen to my kid? That I don't have any opinion and I have to do what he says?" My response is that parents are certainly entitled to their opinion; they should express how they feel and what they regard as the benefits or drawbacks of sports participation. But too often that opinion is not regarded as simply an opinion; it becomes the law. It's used in a coercive way—"You listen to me or else." Even after the parents express their opinions, if the child says, "Well, I still don't want to play," then they should respect his opinion. As Lloyd Percival, the late director of Toronto's Sports and Fitness Institute, wrote:

We must understand that not every youngster *wants* to be involved in high pressure competition. However, he may want to *participate* and should have the opportunity so that he can have fun, keep fit and develop an activity he can enjoy the rest of his life. Parents should not feel their youngsters lack courage and spirit if they don't want to play competitive sport. Perhaps their areas of competitive interest lie in finding a cure for cancer, making money in the stock market or becoming teachers of mathematics.

Most parents try to justify their position by developing excuses or reasons for playing. They may point out that the other youngsters in the neighborhood are playing, or they will suggest that it's important for the child to learn to compete, or that sports is good for one's health and it will "build character" and make him a better person. As I have already discussed, sports has the *potential* to make these and other contributions, but there is no guarantee that any of these benefits will accrue. In fact, if parents force their children to participate—or leave the final decision up to them, but with the strong implication that the child *should* participate—then both sides will lose in the long run. The child will play halfheartedly, just going through the motions, and thus negate any potential benefits that might result from athletics.

One of the tragedies of our sports-obsessed society is the way we measure the male, from kindergarten onward, not so much by his mental aptitudes but by his athletic skills. Novelist Dan Wakefield, a self-admitted nonathlete, wrote in *Women-Sports* magazine about the misery of growing up with no athletic ability "in a society that brainwashes males with the notion that 'manhood' is equivalent to athletic prowess. Getting rid of that concept is inextricably connected with getting rid of the notion that women who enjoy and excel at sport and who want to make a pastime or even a profession of it are not somehow deficient in 'femininity' or aberrant in their behavior."

I realize that there are well-meaning, enlightened parents with a shy, reticent youngster who they feel would enjoy sports and would benefit immeasurably from such a social interaction. Yet they know that without a strong nudge or constant encouragement, the child will never get up the nerve or have the inclination to show up for registration day. "What do we do?" these parents ask.

This is where communication between parent and child is so crucial, and why it is vital for the parents to know their youngster's personality and value structure. In an open family, the parents won't browbeat the child into joining, but rather they will present their "case" for sports and offer their logistical support—the family sedan, money for a uniform and equipment, etc. Then all they can do is let the child make the final decision. If he wants to wait another year or two, until his interests and his self-confidence are likely to have changed, that's hardly a disaster for someone eight or ten years old. In fact, if he waits he may bring a healthier interest to sports and a stronger ability to cope with the pressures than the youngster who already has been competing three or four years.

How to Know If the Child Is Ready for Sports

The child who is not ready to play competitive sports will seem disinterested when the subject is brought up. He will show a degree of inhibition or queasiness and may simply state, "I don't want to play hockey," when his father is standing there with a new pair of skates and a hockey stick. All the father should do is ask why. And if the child doesn't have a reason—"I just don't want to play"—then the sensible father will let the matter drop and not force the child to come up with a reason or to play out of fear or guilt. This is a nightmare for many a boy, who is shamed into playing by an aggressive father who starts questioning his courage, refers to him as a sissy, or tells friends in front of the boy, "No, Johnny's not playing any sports. I guess he's just going to be a mama's boy." (It is interesting that we don't have a corresponding put-down for the girl who doesn't want to compete in sports. She can always escape into her "feminine" defense, while the girl who is the tomboy is the one who must suffer the gibes of others.)

Youngsters, meanwhile, who are ready for sports will give themselves away. They start to ask a lot of questions about sports and talk about their sports heroes. They want technical information, such as how to catch a pass or how to serve the ball. They start to read the sports pages and listen to the games on the radio or beg to go see a sports figure in person. They may show interest in wearing certain kinds of equipment like a baseball cap or a football jersey. They want jerseys with special numbers or colors because they want to identify with their heroes. They start hanging around other youngsters who are also interested in sports.

If the child wants to start playing a sport and is obviously enthused about competing, then the parents should have a discussion with him *on his level* about some of the problems and situations that can arise in athletics. This will help the parents better understand the child's readiness for competition and will alert the child to aspects of sports that he or she may have overlooked or never thought about. This doesn't have to be a deep, penetrating, philosophical discussion, but the parents should encourage the child to talk frankly about such things as:

Why does he (or she) want to participate? Are all of his friends going out? What is he looking forward to? Is he excited or apprehensive?

Is he willing to meet the demands of the sport—the conditioning, the practice, the loss of most free time? Is he *aware* of the amount of time that will be required? Children usually don't stop to think about the fact that participating in a sport will cost them this free time.

Has he thought about what might happen if he gets hurt? Does he already have those fears? What will happen if he sits on the bench? Does he plan to stick with the sport no matter how little he might play?

What are his feelings about competition and the importance of winning? Most children do not realize what the negative effects of losing in a highly competitive environment might be, the disappointment or unhappiness that can result, if not on the part of the child, then certainly in the reactions by parents and coaches. The parents might also point out that the youngster could get chewed out by the coach or punished for poor performances.

Self-Questioning by Parents

Most aspects of a child's personality will be reflected in competitive sports, especially under pressure. If the parents can anticipate how their child will react to competition and stress, they can better cope with the emotions that are aroused during a season. In addition to discussing some of the psychological aspects of sports with their child, the parents should do some crucial self-questioning of their own:

What has led to their child wanting to participate? If the parents have been pushing the idea, they might expect some kind of rebellion or resistance, even if the child agrees to play; children who initiate involvement in sports are likely to have much more interest than if it is initiated by their parents. On the other hand, if the child originated the idea, it might require some type of sacrifice by the parents, such as money for the uniform and equipment, or driving the car to practices and games.

Is the child being realistic about his or her ability? If the child is talented, the sport will probably be fun and relatively easy; if he lacks ability, he may be in for an unhappy experience and may want to quit in midseason. If he is participating just to be with his friends, it might be painful if his friends play and he doesn't play; it might actually cause a split between two friends, as a result of one playing and the other sitting on the bench. This is not an uncommon problem.

How is the child likely to respond to competition? If he is confident and aggressive, he will probably enjoy competition. If he is shy and easily intimidated, he will probably play poorly under pressure. The parents might be embarrassed if their youngster tends to be cowardly, cries whenever he makes a mistake, or throws a temper tantrum when someone tries to correct his technique. Yet if participation in sports really does make a contribution to a child's growth, it will help the child work out problems such as these.

The parents should try to anticipate certain situations. "If our youngster wants to withdraw from sports at any time, what will our reaction be?" Even if their child were a star, would they be likely to give their sanction amicably, without imposing tremendous guilt on the child?

Parents who deny that the child won't be affected emotionally by sports, who shrug their shoulders and say, "That's alright, it's good for him; it will help him grow up," are being unrealistic and insensitive. Those who take this attitude are the ones who sign their child up for a sport and then can't understand why Fenwick suddenly wants to quit two months later, or why sports have made him a nervous wreck. On the other hand, if athletics are properly approached, they can provide a great opportunity for parents and children to form a strong bond of communication while the child is growing as a person and as an athlete.

7

Dealing with the Emotions
of Childhood Sports

THERE WAS A NEWSPAPER cartoon a few years ago that could serve as the epithet for nearly every youngster in organized, competitive sports.

A little boy is playing the outfield and circling under a fly ball. "If I catch the ball," he says, "the manager will love me, my friends will think I'm great, my parents will adore me, and I'll be a hero." Then his buoyant spirits darken. "But if I miss the ball, the manager won't like me, the kids will make fun of me, my parents won't let me in the house, and I'll be a dud."

The ball finally comes down, hits the boy's outstretched glove—and bounces out. In the final panel we see him trudging off the field, shoulders slumped and head bowed. "Six years old," he says, "and already a failure.".

Most parents look upon competitive sports as an activity that will offer good exercise and companionship for their child while providing valuable lessons in competition, teamwork, dedication, and self-discipline. They think their own feelings and reactions have no real effect on their child. If the child also makes it through the season without being seriously injured, the parents will consider the entire venture a success. "Isn't it great that Johnny could play?"

This rosy viewpoint, however, overlooks—even dismisses— the crucial psychological effects of sports, from how the child handles personal failure and defeat to the way he copes with a lack of ability and sitting on the bench. Competitive sports are not a succession of unspoiled pleasures for the young athlete. The fear of injury can create a great deal of anxiety, let alone the painful aspects of contact sports like football and hockey. Demonstrating one's talent before teammates, parents, coaches, and spectators adds further stress—especially when the adults involved have expectations that far exceed the child's physical and psychological maturity. The pressure to win poses additional tension by making the average little athlete constantly fearful of failure, if not on a personal level then as part of a team. Add the differing circumstances of competition, such as a championship game or the final set of a crucial tennis match, and it is easy to see how athletics can be a continual source of anxiety, even for the most talented players. One of the goals of sports participation should be to have the youngster learn to deal with these anxieties in a productive way. But this takes sympathetic, reassuring parents and coaches.

My critics often say, "How can something like winning and losing affect our children? It's good that they compete, even if they lose and shed a few tears." This ignores the fact that many adults, let alone ten-year-old quarterbacks, are unable to handle personal setbacks in sports. In addition, child's play is not the equivalent of adults' play. Games are the child's way of growing up, of developing his personality. If the child fails or suffers sharp disappointments, it can have a strong impact on his emerging psyche, unless he is supported by his coach and his parents.

One reason why the psychological impact of childhood sports is consistently glossed over is that many parents have a tendency to overlook anything that might be a symptom. Or they alter the symptom in their heads. If, for example, they see their child crying after a loss they tend to think that it's good for the child to learn about adversity and fighting back. Conversely, the child may hide the fact that he cried after losing the game—for fear of being ridiculed by his father—or that he was injured, for fear of having to miss the next game.

On a deeper level, the child may come home from a game and seem relatively sullen and sad. He doesn't say anything but goes to his room and stays there for an hour. He may have lost the game, he may have been a substitute and didn't get a chance to play, he may have played poorly and is depressed even though the team won. Instead of discussing it with the child and helping him deal with his disappointment, the parents will say, "Aw, he's okay. It's just one of those things. It's only Little League." What if the same thing happened to the husband who didn't get the big contract or the promotion or who got chewed out by the boss? How would he feel if his wife just shrugged her shoulders and told him, "That's okay, dear, it's just your job. It's only a passing thing"?

The same proportional pressures affect the young athlete, and parents must respond in a corresponding manner. There's relatively little difference, theoretically, between being a Little Leaguer and being a major league baseball player. We build stadiums for our children, manicure their diamonds, enforce the rules, keep statistics and standings, pick All-Star teams, and send them to the play-offs. These same early pressures exist in Pop Warner football, where players are "drafted," study game films, memorize plays, and sometimes travel out of state for road games or "bowl" appearances. In neither sport is losing a laughing matter.

Following are the major areas that can produce emotional stress in childhood sports, and some thoughts on how parents can best help their children cope.

Losing

"Soon fades the spell, soon comes the night,
Say will it not be then the same,
Whether we played the black or white,
Whether we lost or won the game?"

—Lord Macaulay

Nearly every parent has been faced with the awkward, sometimes distressing situation of having their child in tears after losing the crucial baseball game or important tennis match. What the youngster needs more than anything is emotional support. He needs somebody to put an arm around him and say, "Johnny, that's alright. That was a tough game. I know how you feel." There's no magic liniment that parents can rub in to ease the hurt. Sometimes, however, just having the parents there watching the game and being around afterwards will be all that's necessary. The most destructive thing a parent can do is punish the child for losing, either verbally or physically. Losing is painful enough; there is no need to heap more misery on the child by indulging in the "I told you so" game: "I told you that you weren't practicing hard enough. I told you that you would lose if you didn't start going to bed early. I told you they would beat you if you didn't listen to the coach." These are common means of parents' adding to an already painful situation. No child wants to hear such statements, when he is already hurting from the sting of a defeat. It is a poor way for the parents to establish superiority. In fact, it is possible that they are undermining the opportunity to establish greater communication and rapport with their child. Equally cruel is for parents to use this approach when dealing with a youngster's minor injury— "Brush it off, it's not that bad." Well, you can't deny feeling miserable. If you could brush off disappointment and personal conflicts, mental health would be no problem.

Parents should instead emphasize more positive approaches,

based on the understanding that every mature person must learn to adjust to failure. A person doesn't have to be happy or content to lose, but the fact remains that everybody fails in some things sooner or later. The question is how to adjust, and there's no better place to learn this than in sports, where everything happens so fast that it can be forgotten in a short period of time.

Parents (and coaches) should keep certain things in mind when faced by a child who has lost or failed in sports.

Don't ignore him or give him the silent treatment. Let him know that it's painful, and that you understand how it feels to lose. But remind him that winning and losing are a part of life and that a loss is not the end of the world. One of the beauties of sports is that you can play again tomorrow, or in another week; it's sad today but tomorrow it will be a little different.

Don't give the child the impression that he is personally a failure. Losing doesn't mean that he is a lesser person. He may have worked and hustled and been just as talented as the winner, but society says that someone has to win and someone has to lose, no matter how fine the line between them may be.

Be understanding, but realistic. Don't let the child make excuses, and don't try to make him feel better by offering him excuses. Remember that the opponent was simply better *today*, if not yesterday or next week.

Instead of looking upon failure as a complete, dismal blackout, parents should talk from a positive, encouraging standpoint: "What did you learn from this game? What information did you pick up that can help you later?" Losing, in fact, may be more valuable to a person's growth than winning—*if* the losing is seen in its proper perspective and you lost while giving your best. It may be that you don't learn too much from winning; there's less of an adjustment, and it can obscure personal faults. But losing may provide a more realistic appraisal of what's going on. It forces a person to rethink what he is doing: "Maybe I'm not as good as I thought I was. I'd better find out what I'm doing wrong."

Emphasize the philosophy that the true test of an individual's competitiveness is his ability to handle defeat maturely. Praise the youngster who can lose gracefully and with courage. In terms of personal growth, that should be seen as a form of winning. Former UCLA basketball player Tommy Curtis remembered that when he was fourteen his team lost a game, and he was so down on himself that he "cried like a baby" and walked twenty-one miles home. His mother told him, "You won't have control over what happens most of the time, but you will have the opportunity to dictate how you react."

The parents should be concerned about what losing means to the child, not to them. Some parents, for instance, will interpret the child's failure as a rejection of them. This may be true in some cases, but mostly it's a case where the child simply did not succeed. Parents who feel rejected by the child's failure will proceed to punish the child, as if to retaliate for what the child has done to them.

Defeat should never be such a crushing matter that it ruins the weekend. The child must know that if he loses, or has a bad game or performs poorly, he can still come in the front door and his parents are going to be happy to see him. Regardless of the outcome, be it a baseball game or a swimming meet, the parents and child should be able to communicate in a pleasant way. The child is in trouble when the outcome becomes a significant factor in the eyes of the parents.

After a loss, parents should rarely evaluate performance, but rather should reward physical involvement: the effort, working hard, putting in the time and sticking with it. If the child performed his best or worked up to his potential, he shouldn't have to apologize or feel guilty about losing. The key concern should be: did he still have fun playing the game? Did he enjoy himself?

Parents and young athletes alike should realize that it is entirely possible to gain and maintain self-respect—and still lose—by admitting, "This is the best I can do." Just to say

"Let's face it—I'm less talented" is a healthy form of adjustment. "I can still figure out math and play the piano; I just don't have as much talent in this one sport." Unfortunately, the American culture has built so much guilt into losing that the person who tries to make a healthy adjustment to it—like cracking jokes in the midst of a losing streak—is thought to be a lousy competitor, if not a little crazy. We incorporate this futilistic feeling into the fiber of the child's personality as he's growing up. The child should be free to take honest pride in winning. But he should also be allowed to learn to cope with defeat.

The Substitute

Another prevailing myth in sports is that a hardworking substitute will come out of the experience with a stronger character. On the contrary, unless a child is extremely mature or unless he gets a great deal of support from his parents, being a substitute will affect him adversely. I have only known of one preadolescent competitor who was content being a substitute, and that was because he had been rejected by a number of other groups and so didn't mind being a substitute, just as long as he belonged. He was also extremely awkward so just being kept on the team was satisfying.

We don't give much thought to the poor little guy on the bench, his disillusionment and his sense of futility. Dr. Bill Hammer and I conducted a study that showed that the athlete who suffers the most, and often loses his motivation, is the substitute. The reality he faces is that things rarely get any better during the season. For one thing, he doesn't get a chance to improve his skills; those who play all the time keep drawing further ahead of him. He grows progressively more disillusioned and more isolated, especially on a winning team, where he is frustrated at not being able to contribute. On a losing team, ironically, the substitute can always cling to the hope of playing, while feeling, "I can play better than those guys."

Another painful aspect of being a substitute is the fact that the child's presence on the bench is an obvious sign of his being somewhat inferior. If he were more talented, he would be on the first string. He must face this embarrassment not only with his peers, who are clearly aware of it, but with his parents as well. If, in addition, he is highly competitive, being on the bench can serve as a personal letdown, because he has not attained goals he may have set. He may appear somewhat depressed during the season because of this. To add to the problem, this depression may carry over to other phases of his life. For example, he may begin to do poorly in school, particularly if school is not that important to him. There may be a tendency to avoid his friends, especially those who are on the first string, simply because they may ask sensitive questions or poke fun at his practicing with the scrubs. If he is also quizzed by his parents as to why he is not starting, or if they begin to push him to practice more, the problem becomes even greater.

To make matters worse, as sociologist Dr. Jon Brower observed after studying a North Hollywood, California, baseball program (boys ages eight to fourteen) for nearly a year: "It is the poor players who get the brunt of the coaches' displeasure and thus suffer the most. Like most young competitors, their athletic involvement constitutes a major part of their lives; they have fewer alternative activities than adults and thus if they are poor players they define themselves as defective human beings."

There are several important ways in which parents can help their child effectively handle the role of a substitute. It is vital that they let their child know that they are not judging him as a person based on his playing ability, and that they love him because of the kind of person he is. Unfortunately, many parents respond as if it were a personal insult that their child is a substitute, no matter how uncoordinated he might be. This simply compounds the child's guilt and misery.

If the child comes home and is obviously disappointed, it is extremely important to empathize with him. If he says, "I didn't get a chance to play again today," the parent shouldn't tell him, "Well, the other kids are better than you" or "Life is like that, it's tough." The parent should say something like, "It must embarrass you not to play, and I know how the feeling is. You kinda feel left out. If I were sitting on the bench it would hurt my feelings, too. But I'm really proud of you the way you're sticking it out." Sometimes the parent doesn't have to say anything; he can just pat the youngster on the back or be a good listener. The parent should also make an effort to see that the child gets a chance to play in some way, such as in a pickup game after work once a week with some of the other youngsters who aren't playing. Or the parent could offer to help the child improve by throwing extra batting practice or taking him out to the basketball court and working on his shooting.

Parents can help preempt the problem before the season even begins by telling the child, "Everybody has different abilities and different talents. That's part of the game. You may not get the chance to play as much as you might want to, but we're happy that you want to go out for the team. No matter what happens, we're behind you." Don't discourage the child by being derogatory; don't destroy his motivation. The valuable part is that he wants to take part, he wants to give the sport a try, even though the odds may be against his playing very much. That is why the process—the trying—must be rewarded, rather than waiting until he does well, which may be improbable.

Once again, that old nemesis—the emphasis on winning—is what leads to most of the substitute problems on a childhood sports level. For example, there was a Pop Warner football coach in Los Angeles who used only his best players in one particularly close, important game. The team still lost, and afterwards the coach was confronted by a group of angry parents whose youngsters had not played. The coach was later quoted in *Los Angeles* magazine, in which he defended his position and criticized the parents: "That's not what Pop Warner is all about. The kids want to win, too, and if you play everybody and keep losing, it's demoralizing. The point about all these organized sports for kids is, if you can't have fun, forget it." Yes, but fun for whom—the coach and the twenty-two starters? What about the other eleven boys on the bench, one-third of the team? Isn't it demoralizing for them to keep coming out to practices and to the games but seldom getting to play? A letter to the *Miami Herald* from the mother of a Little League football player presented a poignant protest in this regard. She wrote that her son's coach screamed at referees, screamed into the faces of the boys, and, worst of all, allowed only twelve of his eighteen players to play. "The other boys sat on the bench for the second week in a row, not being allowed in for even one play," she said. "These are eleven-year-olds who give up every night of the week to practice, come home late, tired, dirty, hungry, but with the thought it will be worth it when they play on Saturday. Ha."

I will discuss in more detail later why every childhood sports league should require the coach to play every youngster in every game, and more than just token appearances. Some league officials and coaches might be surprised to learn that most parents could be in favor of having all the players see as much action as possible. In 1974 I surveyed one hundred parents and coaches in a San Jose Little League, and the overwhelming majority of parents preferred to have their youngsters play regularly for a loser than ride the bench for a winner. A similar study of Pop Warner football players in the Colorado–New Mexico area showed that almost three-quarters of them would rather see action with a losing team than sit on the bench with a winner.

Peer Group Troubles

Parents are sometimes faced with a situation where the other players are giving their child a rough time because of his clumsiness or general ineptitude. They ridicule him and taunt him, and he doesn't know how to respond. The most important thing here is for the child to know that his parents are concerned about him. They should talk to him about his feelings and let him know that they understand. They should ask him why he thinks the other players give him such a rough time. Perhaps the child's personality is contributing to the problem; he may be an alibier or a constant complainer, or he may be insulting to the other players. If the parents have a good relationship with the coach, they could ask him to provide an insight into what is happening, since he sees the interplay going on during a game or at practice. The parents should let the coach know they're concerned. Is there anything they can do? What might change the situation? Sometimes the parents can ease the tension by inviting the whole team over to the house for hamburgers. The other ballplayers may realize that Fenwick isn't such a bad kid after all; they might like him a little bit more. Above all, however, the child needs to know he at least has his parents behind him. He needs to know they support him.

Fear of Getting Hurt

Many children have the very natural fear of getting hurt when they take up a sport that has repeated physical contact or is fraught with potential dangers. For instance, every Pop Warner team has the little guy who doesn't like to get hit, who's not very aggressive, but whose father is going to make him a football player. Young hockey players everywhere are afraid to scuffle for the puck amidst flailing sticks or to be knocked against the boards by an aggressive opponent. In individual sports, the athlete must overcome similar fears while learning to ski the downhill or dive from the ten-meter platform or perform on the balance beam in gymnastics.

Children in these situations need emotional support. They need to know that their parents and the coach understand their fears and will not reject them if they cry or back away from danger. One of the recurring problems in baseball, for example, is how to relax the player who is terrified of coming up to the plate against a fast pitcher, especially one with control problems. A mother once asked me for advice on how to cope with this dilemma, which involved her baseball-crazy husband and their young son, who was just starting Little League and was terribly "gun-shy" up at the plate, jumping away from every pitch. The father was a pushy, tough-minded person whose "solution" was to take his son out to the baseball field and make him stand at home plate with a bat while he hit him with baseballs. "It's gonna make him tough," he told his wife. "This is the only way he'll learn to stand in there." Obviously this was crazy behavior. Trying to browbeat bravery into a youngster only reinforces and increases his existing fears. But this was typical, albeit to the extreme, of the insensitive approaches taken by many parents and coaches in trying to calm the fears of young athletes. They try to either shame the child—"Don't be a sissy"—or provide false hopes—"Don't be afraid, it's not going to hurt you." The latter is make-believe thinking. I mean, there's no denying the fact that getting hit by a hardball is painful, sometimes even injurious.

What the adult should do is talk to the youngster about fear and recognize the fact that the child is afraid. Just discussing the problem will help alleviate worries: "I know what it's like to get hit by the ball. It hurts. I wish it didn't have to be a part of the game. But really, it happens very seldom. If you're alert up there, you can jump out of the way almost every time. The pitcher is *trying* to get the ball over the plate—he's not aiming at you—so just concentrate on hitting the ball." When the youngster is first learning how to hit, the adults should use a softball or a whiffle ball so that the youngster knows he won't be hurt if he stands in at the plate. He should be allowed to gain confidence in his ability to hit the ball before he moves up to a hardball and faster speeds. The youngster who knows he can hit the ball, or at least make repeated contact, will soon have the confidence to concentrate on hitting rather than on his fear of getting hurt.

The Child Who Wants to Quit

In most highly competitive and involved families, the pressure on young athletes is not only to win, but not to quit, especially if they have talent and a "future" in the sport. In such families it is difficult, if not impossible, for the child to go up to his parents and say, "I've decided to quit." His parents just aren't going to accept that decision gracefully, no matter how long the child might have suffered, enduring a sport he no longer enjoyed while trying to get up enough courage to face condemnation by his parents. Competitive parents will almost always take a strong stand—"If you start something you have to see it through"—and will argue that quitters never learn to face the real world. To drop out of football, especially, is to admit an unmanly weakness.

However, as Dr. Bryant Cratty writes in *Children and Youth in Competitive Sports*: "There is no data which indicates that a child who is not willing to endure the physical rigors of sports is likely to fail in tasks involving intellectual or artistic persistence. . . . Indeed, if the child has personality traits that do not suit him for competitive sports, he may be suited for participation in activities which may result in more worthwhile contributions to himself and to others. In other areas he may display competencies which may endure into adulthood more than do sports skills."

If the parents and the child wage long, heated arguments over the question of continued participation in a sport, the child can never win. Even if the parents finally give in, the child will be left with so much guilt that he will wish he were back on the team. Instead of producing such a confrontation, parents should allow a reevaluation time to sit down with the child and discuss in a positive way why he wants to quit. Since most families consider quitting a form of losing, the parents should remember all the ramifications. The child needs support, not a browbeating, and the parents need to explore his reasons, not simply dismiss him as a quitter. For example, is the coach riding him too hard? Does he resent being on the bench most of the time? Does he feel left out? Do the other players make fun of him? Is he embarrassed because his friends are on the first team and he's a substitute? If he's a starter, why has his interest in the sport diminished? Perhaps the child is hurting physically but he doesn't want to admit it and this is his indirect way of doing it. Maybe he never really wanted to participate in the first place, despite having good talent, but he didn't want to disappoint his parents, or he's afraid of what his friends will think.

Parents will never know these things until they talk to their child. The child may, in fact, be going through such a painful experience that the decision to quit may be entirely reasonable. But if the parents persist in forcing him to finish out the season, they can expect to create more problems and produce deep-seated negative attitudes. For the child it may be like developing school phobia; he has to go to the ball field and it's going to be very painful. He will find ways to fudge. He will play so poorly and show such obvious disinterest that he should have stayed home anyway. His reaction will be, "If I'm playing just to please my parents, then I'll just go through the motions." The parents, in fact, are teaching him to slough off.

Many times the pressures on a young athlete can build up to such a point that the youngster indirectly, but very purposely, takes his frustrations out on his parents. I've had athletes tell me that they purposely played poorly because they wanted to be thrown off the team; they couldn't take the conflict with their father any longer. I knew of an outstanding high school pitcher who started on the mound in the championship game.

The stands were filled with scouts and he knew his father was there, a smart-ass, cocky type who was loudly arrogant about his son's ability. The boy proceeded to throw the first ten pitches nowhere near the plate—in the dirt, into the backstop. He later admitted to his school counselor that he did it intentionally to pay back his father, because his hurt was so deep and so great and he had carried it for so long.

Another example occurred in the San Jose area, where the father was a former wrestler and his son was wrestling on the high school team. The father would get so engrossed that he would literally become his son during a match, going through all the motions, the empathy, the agony, as he watched from the stands. Then came a crucial qualifying match for the state championships. Late in the match the son got in a tough spot and pulled some blunder, and there in this silent gym the father lost control of himself. He started shouting instructions at the top of his lungs and putting his son down. When the boy finally got loose he walked over to his corner, pulled on his sweat pants, and left the ring. He never wrestled again.

The decision to drop out of a sport may not come until the season is over, and the reasons may surprise those parents who fail to realize that organized sports are not the ultimate joy of childhood for many youngsters. I knew one boy who played on two winning Pop Warner teams, but he realized that he was never going to be that good, so why continue to go out and sit on the bench? He quit because he liked other things and it seemed sensible to shift his focus of attention; playing football was a chore, like carrying out the garbage.

I once talked to a father who had wanted his son to learn to compete and to be successful. So he talked Jimmy into going out for the junior high basketball team. The coach was just out of college and he had the players come in every day for a rough, two-hour practice. He really put them through the grinder, but they won their league and Jimmy was one of the leading scorers. His father told me about this in a very proud fashion, and the implication was "It's wonderful that my boy had this sports experience." Then he admitted, "I asked Jimmy, 'Well, how did you like basketball? Are you looking forward to next year?' And he said, 'Well, Dad, I'm not going out next year.' When I asked him why, he said, 'Jeez, that's a lot of work and it took all my time. I always had to stay after school for practice and I couldn't play with my friends, or watch TV.' "

Clearly these things were more important to the boy than playing basketball all winter. Many parents would argue that since he had athletic ability, he should have been forced to compete. But look at it from the child's point of view; he went to school and he did his work; he was entitled to his free time. Forcing him to compete would be unfair.

Perceptive parents can usually sense ahead of time when a sport is beginning to affect their child in a negative way, and can help the child wrestle with the problem before it leads to a confrontation over quitting.

For example, the child who starts discovering that a sport just isn't fun anymore will reveal a number of symptoms. He will find it hard to concentrate on the sport. He will cease to speak excitedly about what he is doing, and will lose his eagerness to go to practice. He may even feign sickness or act hurt in order to get out of going. If he's a substitute or has been playing poorly, he may try to avoid his friends who do play—and who used to be his close pals. He may no longer even want to participate informally with his brothers or his father. He begins to find fault with his teammates and tries to blame the coach for whatever problems he is having in the sport. If he plays poorly he may go home and hide in his room. If you try to talk about practice, and it happens that he has just been benched, instead of telling you he may begin to cry. In severe cases there might be anxiety symptoms such as fidgeting and nail biting or even nausea and nightmares, all associated with participation in sports—and affected to a large degree by the amount of pressure being exerted on the home front.

If the parents created the situation in the first place, by

strongly encouraging the child to sign up for the sport, they will only compound the problem by trying to ignore these emotional symptoms. Again, what the parents must do is talk to the child at some length about his participation. If the symptoms persist, or a number of them intensify, then the parents should even encourage the child to withdraw. At the least, they should always leave the door open for the child to make that decision on his own, and without guilt.

8

Emotional Child Abuse

If a child lives with criticism,
He learns to condemn.
If a child lives with hostility,
He learns to fight.
If a child lives with ridicule,
He learns to be shy.
If a child lives with shame,
He learns to feel guilty.
If a child lives with tolerance,
He learns to be patient.
If a child lives with encouragement,
He learns confidence.
If a child lives with praise,
He learns to appreciate.
If a child lives with fairness,
He learns justice.
If a child lives with security,
He learns to have faith.
If a child lives with approval,
He learns to like himself.

If a child lives with acceptance and friendship,
He learns to find love in the world.
                —Dorothy Law Nolte:
                "Children Learn What They Live"

Child abuse is ordinarily defined in physical terms, when a child is beaten or tortured in some way by his parents. Every year thousands of children—that we know of—are abused in this manner by parents who are seeking to discipline or punish their child or to show anger that the child was ever born. Obviously this is a tragic "method" of child rearing. Yet there is another parent-child relationship that can have equally devastating results psychologically, and that is *emotional child abuse,* isolated or pervasive actions by parents that can shatter a child's emotional growth. If this abuse is coupled with the built-in pressures of competitive sports, it can nearly destroy a child's psychological growth.

One problem with emotional child abuse is that it is sometimes almost impossible to detect; the child is not cut or bruised or banged up. The child may be just as crippled psychologically, but nobody can tell the parents, "You did it right here." What's more, if a child has a broken arm you can take him to the doctor. But if his self-esteem has been undermined by his parents, you can't send him to a self-confidence clinic.

Parents would never think of binding a child's legs so they wouldn't grow. Yet they will straitjacket their child's emotional growth without even realizing the damage they are doing. Emotional abuse can occur in several ways.

It can occur when, directly or indirectly, a child is coerced into athletics without volunteering and before he is ready physically or psychologically. His parents may want him to do the things they always wanted to do but were unable to do. Now that the opportunities are available, they don't want their child to miss out. To carry out the parents' hopes and expectations is a tremendous burden even for the most gifted and ambitious child.

Parents can also frustrate a child by setting unrealistic and constantly shifting goals for him to achieve in order to gain their approval. Then they can undermine his self-esteem by constantly deprecating his efforts rather than offering praise and support.

In a family where the parents make it clear that they don't tolerate quitters, the child who wants to quit might force himself to stay out for the sport and continue to suffer rather than face their wrath. They may not even be aware of what their child is going through; they are pushing and encouraging his participation when all he wants to do is stay home with his friends.

What leads parents to treat their children in this fashion, whether it's over schoolwork, sports participation, or other extracurricular activities? Studies of physical child abusers indicate several common characteristics. First, these parents view their children as possessions—"This is my kid and he'll do what I say, or else." They feel they "own" their children and that child rearing is not something to share with them. Secondly, they feel that physical punishment is the only way to enforce respect. Third, they were invariably abused themselves as children. They have no other model. They feel they have a perfect right to belt their children—"that's the way I was raised and that's the only way they're going to learn." And fourth, they have unrealistic expectations about the child's behavior or performance.

These traits should hold true for emotional child abuse as well. If you were emotionally abused as a child, how are you going to be able to differentiate? The only hope for your children is if you are determined not to raise them the way you were raised.

By browbeating their child into carrying out their wishes and dreams parents can destroy much more than the child's temporary self-confidence. They can produce long-term personality problems. For instance, the child may end up being very flaky, that is, unable to handle his emotions. Or he may become a bully or overly aggressive, if he learns to cope with frustration by beating up people. On the other hand, he may be easily intimidated, depending on his own personality and the approach taken by his parents. He may also become very dependent, unable to do anything without the help of somebody else. Or he may never be able to accept losing as a growth experience.

Parents who are guilty of emotional child abuse have interfered with the normal maturing process. They've destroyed the child's domain of growing up and may have helped drive him away from what could have been beneficial throughout his life—an active involvement in sports and an appreciation for physical activity. Of course, trying to relate the effect of emotional child abuse and the child's participation in sports to long-range personality growth is a difficult, if not impossible, task. The child is obviously strongly influenced by parental reactions to his activities in school and around home. But given the widespread mania for childhood sports, and the corresponding emphasis that many parents place on winning and success, emotional abuse will have a very damaging impact.

Family Influences

Families have certain value structures and certain predictable behavior patterns. Some families put a premium on competition, others abhor it. Some families want to be supersophisticated, others tend to be down-to-earth. Yet certain family "styles" more than others are likely to have a strong negative influence on children, especially the young athlete.

One is the Perfectionistic Family. Children who grow up in this situation can never really win. Whatever they do, they have to do perfectly. Their bedrooms have to be spic-and-span. Their clothes have to be neat. They have to get A's in school. Everything is scheduled for them—study time, TV time, meal time, play time.

The child who takes up sports under these circumstances has got to be a winner and work towards being absolutely perfect. Perfectionistic parents generally have a high concept of their family. They find it difficult to accept an average athlete. If their child can barely walk to home plate without tripping over his feet, it's embarrassing for them to go down to the Little League field and discover that the flunky, dirty-faced kid next door is the best player on the team. The perfectionistic parents will think, "We're obviously better than the Smiths," and now their own clumsy child becomes a source of agony. They're torn between taking him out of Little League and keeping him there for his own enjoyment but just not showing up at the games. In many cases they will work him unmercifully to get him to be "perfect," to fit the family image. The poor child, meanwhile, feels guilty that he has disappointed his parents by failing to become a "star."

Another environment that can produce emotional child abuse is that of the Authoritarian Family. This type of family revolves primarily around power. Who's in charge? Who's running the show? The parent who holds the upper hand—it can be either the father or the mother—has got to have the final word. Parents like this produce a phenomenal amount of guilt in sports, because whatever they say has to be accepted and the child has to carry it through. If the child is in a situation where the father's message is clearly "You make the team!" *Not* to make the team is a violation of father's demands, which can evoke guilt as well as a sense of fear. Memories of spankings and other forms of punishment come flashing back, and the child can easily begin to think of himself as a failure.

If a child grows up in a family where the father has to be right every time, then all the doubt, the questioning, the unsureness have to be on the child's part. In authoritarian families where the father is the strong figure, often there is a tendency for the child to overidolize his father. Father has been so much of a standard, and so good, that the child can never overcome the feeling that his father will always be superior to him, no matter what he does—unless the father is supportive, kind, considerate, and strong and helps the child work it out. What usually happens, however, is that the child always has to fail or at least to be less than his father. He may, in fact, be very apologetic if he outdoes his father, just as there's often a resentment on the father's part to be outdone by his son.

A further area of emotional abuse by parents concerns the status of the nonathlete in a family where emphasis is put on sports achievement. Parents need to be aware that their less talented children lose all the way around. The athlete in the family is given most of the attention and receives most of the accolades, and the nonathlete is neglected. In time the nonathlete may begin to feel unloved and unimportant, as if he had nothing to offer.

Parents in this situation should keep track of the time they spend with each child in the family, and make an active effort to give equal time to the child who is nonathletic. Often there's the tendency to neglect the nonathlete simply because he doesn't have an activity that consumes his time in such a conspicuous way as organized sports. For instance, if one boy in the family is playing Little League, the parents will happily go to all his games (and then rehash the games at dinner). But how many parents will spend the equivalent two or three hours with the child who is trying to grow a vegetable garden? How often will parents spend long, uninterrupted hours with the child who loves to read, discussing the books he has just finished?

If parents do make a point of setting aside special time to go to the zoo or the park with the nonathlete, they will only compound the problem if they take the athlete along, because then he is getting double attention. Similarly, the parents should never force the nonathlete to go to the Little League game or swimming meet, because that's like rubbing it in. He will only feel more resentment, unless he can simply accept his lack of talent and go to the game and enjoy it anyway. All too often, however, he just doesn't communicate that he feels left out, that he feels hurt by the actions of his parents.

The Mother's Influence

In chapter 6 I pointed out how the mother's sensitivities can often be a tempering influence on the sports-crazy father. Unfortunately, our society has also produced a great many mothers who are ill equipped to deal rationally with many of the realities of competitive sports for children.

Women can be just as competitive as men, sometimes more so. They live in a competitive environment, they see their husbands compete, and they compete in their own way with the house next door or with the other mothers on the block. Yet most women have never been in a position to work out their competitive spirit in sports. High school gym classes for girls in past years provided barely more than modern dance and volleyball, and only a handful of women participated in organized athletic programs.

As a result, many mothers use their children to work out their own competitive urge vicariously. When a youngster signs up for a team, the mother generally becomes more involved than the father. She usually makes all the arrangements and drives her child to practice sessions and games. She observes her offspring being evaluated along with all the other players. As her own competitive needs begin to surface, she identifies more and more with her child and his success. It is extremely difficult, however, to identify with someone if you have never been in his shoes. If you've never played football, you have no idea what it's like to get hit so hard that you forget your name. If you've never played baseball, you have no idea what it's like to get hit by a fast-pitched ball and then have to face the same pitcher two innings later. It looks so simple to go faster, to make the tackle, to sink the basket.

This happens to many mothers. Discouraged from involvement in competition, particularly competitive sports, when they were young, they find it easy to slough off pain or defeat vicariously. Their child becomes a pawn for their emotional needs. Most mothers don't realize the pressures they can build up on their child or the damage that can result from their being punitive because the child fails to live up to expectations. The mother looks at all the time she has invested and all the money it has cost for the swim club or the ice hockey equipment, and if the child doesn't make the team, or just rides the bench, it's as though the mother had failed too. It's hard for her to accept the fact that her child just wasn't good enough. After all she did, all that effort, the child should have made it. Most mothers find it very difficult to mask their disappointment, and so the poor child feels even worse because of guilt. (It should be stressed, of course, that these things can also hold true with many fathers. They respond the same way in many cases.)

Furthermore, a mother (or father) who has not competed in sports or who has not reached her personal expectation in or out of athletics will often make demands of a youngster that are higher than he or she is capable of achieving, simply because the mother can't identify with the sport or comprehend what it requires of the child. Some cases I have known indicate, in fact, that mother is more rejecting than father in the face of failure, and that father is more sympathetic. One of the girls who swam for the U.S. Olympic team told me, "When I'm out of town for a swimming meet and I call home, I just pray that my father answers the phone."

"Why?" I asked her.

"Because if my mother answers the phone she wants to know my times, how all the other girls did, am I getting enough sleep, what foods am I eating, what am I doing with my free time? She's worse than the coach."

Her father, on the other hand, was supportive, understanding, and concerned about how she felt and what she was going through.

I have heard this complaint time and again, where the

mother is the one who pushes. I think that those fathers who have gone through competitive sports and who compete in their profession every day are more empathetic in some cases, especially with a daughter. After a loss, they're more likely to say, "Look, I know it's tough, but you'll do okay."

I don't like to be heavy on mothers. I'm the first to admit that our male-dominated society produced many of these problems by denying women their fair chance to compete in any realm, especially athletically. This is why I'm such a strong advocate of girls and women being involved in sports at all levels. We need to give them equal opportunities, while breaking down the male—and female—stereotypes that still inhibit their full involvement. An active participation in competitive and participatory sports will make girls not only healthier women but also better mothers. By going through the emotional and physical rigors of childhood and teenage sports, girls today should be far more enlightened than many of their mothers were when they come to deal with their child's sporting psyche.

Positive Versus Negative Reinforcement

Parents should carefully examine the method of punishment and reward within their family, since this will be reflected in how they deal with their young athlete. I feel that an emphasis on positive reinforcement will lead to a sound parent-child relationship, while a heavy-handed, insensitive approach by the parents will only contribute to emotional child abuse.

Positive reinforcement is a method used in a technique called behavioral modification, in which you reward the child with something that is meaningful whenever he exhibits proper behavior. There is a tendency for the behavior that is rewarded to occur more often. By the same token, if certain unfavorable behavior patterns are ignored, or punished, they will tend to decrease in frequency. Children particularly respond to positive reinforcement. The reward certainly doesn't have to be a materialistic object like candy or a toy, but preferably a little affection or a kind word. All they want is a little recognition for what they are trying to achieve or for what they have done right or performed well. Yet so many parents do just the opposite: they punish their child whenever anything goes wrong, but ignore those occasions when the child exhibits good behavior. (Extensive work has been done in this area by Dr. Brent Rushall at Dalhousie University, Nova Scotia.)

There is a stereotypic attitude among many people that psychologists are against discipline. "You guys are very softheaded," they will say. "You don't believe in discipline, you let people run free." But that is not my philosophy at all. I believe that life has limits and dangers, and that one has to learn what they are. It's not a question of whether we should have limits or not, but of how we attempt to have those limits learned. That's the key. Negative reinforcement may be useful when trying to keep a youngster from running into the street or playing with lethal weapons. But sports are not a life-and-death situation. The young athlete is usually there voluntarily, to some degree. He or she enjoys being there and is usually willing to cooperate. To punish this child unnecessarily only detracts from his natural spontaneity and enjoyment of the sport.

Unfortunately, punishment is used as a motivational force by many parents, and they can build in tremendous guilt for not achieving. Many parents like to seize on a losing situation as an opportunity to teach their children a lesson, by using failure as an excuse to work them harder. After a loss, for example, father may take junior back to the playing field and drill him for another hour, to prove to him that he needs to take things more seriously. What actually may be happening is that there is a need on the father's part to punish junior because junior is making him angry in other areas, or junior has embarrassed him by not performing well, or junior has let the family down by not being a winner, etc., etc. This punishing method can cause a parent to lose a child little by little.

I once interviewed a female swimmer who revealed that whenever she swam poorly, her parents would punish her so severely that she was frightened of losing. Like a self-fulfilling prophecy, her fear of doing badly interfered with her concentration and she was swimming progressively slower. Her parents had arranged the interview with me, and I was supposed to tell her how to perform better. But once I realized how deeply ingrained her fears were, all I could do was empathize with her and let her know that I was aware of the pain she was going through. When I tried to explain the problem to her parents, they denied it; they saw it as totally her fault, and said that she was just creating excuses.

On another occasion I was presented with the case of a female swimmer who was a ragged performer. One of my students charted her times in races as well as time trials. Interestingly, after every time she swam well, she would swim poorly. One week, in fact, her all-time best was followed by her all-time poorest. In going back through her history, we learned that her success times were invariably tied to a subtle punishment by her parents. Instead of rewarding her by saying, "What a swim! That was terrific! We're really proud of you," her parents would scold her—"See what you can do? Now if you can only do that tomorrow!" And tomorrow was always these deep plunges on the chart. The girl was never able to resolve this conflict with her parents.

I always urge parents to realize how success can unconsciously be tied to punishment, and how they can create negative reinforcement without being aware of it. For instance, youngsters will do well in practice and their parents will make them almost promise to do well in the meet or in the next game—"See, you *know* you can do it!" And that's punishment, because the child doesn't know if he really can do it the next time or ever again.

When we interview youngsters and discover that they are tender-minded and lacking in emotional control, we suspect they've been subjected to punishment rather than rewards.

These youngsters are so oversensitive about failure and criticism that everything is interpreted as punishment. The parents—and coach—should know this, because the poor athlete is already so busy punishing himself that he doesn't need any outside agitator. The fact that the child still manages to "win" is hardly an excuse for intimidating, domineering, unyielding parents. And if he loses or rides the bench while being handled in this manner, then he's a double loser.

9

Communication and
Competition within the Family

MANY OF THE PROBLEMS in childhood sports could be short-circuited if there were open communication between parents and their young athletes. This communication, as we have seen, should begin when both sides sift through the reasons for, and the emotions behind, an involvement in sports. Once participation begins, if parents expect to maintain a positive, healthy interaction with their child they must stay "athletically acquainted." This involves a continual evaluation of the youngster's attitude towards sports and competition— but on a deeper level than batting averages, swimming times, or proficiency on the balance beam. The parents must stay *emotionally* in tune with the child, not only in order to strengthen their relationship but in order to be more aware of problems resulting from sports participation that might not be physically apparent.

Even if only through discussions at the dinner table with the child, the parents should strive to understand the degree to which he is absorbed in sports.

Is the child having fun? Does he continue to be enthusiastic about baseball or has his interest waned? He might like one part of the game but not another. He might like to talk about hitting, but it might be hard for him to talk about playing the outfield because he makes a lot of errors there. Perhaps he would rather play another sport.

The child's fears may be an indication—direct or indirect—that the sport is not all that much fun. If the sport is football or hockey, the child might admit that he is still afraid of tackling or getting hit by the other players; in baseball he might be "gun-shy" when he goes up to the plate. He might talk about how nervous or frightened he gets before competition. A case of butterflies in the stomach is one thing—a fairly normal occurrence that disappears once competition is under way. But if the child gets physically sick because of the buildup of tension, then obviously the pressures are too much. Vomiting before the game is part of pro football's mystique, a sign of how much the game means to the player, but it's nothing to be proud of on the childhood level. It's an indication that the child is not yet ready to handle the pressure—or the sport. (It is also a sign, as we shall see in chapter 12, that the coach should be investigated for placing such emotional importance on the competition at hand.)

Another measure of the child's enjoyment will be reflected by his (or her) attitude towards competition. The child may not feel that competition is important. He may simply enjoy participating in the game and not really pay much attention to the score. He may even have negative feelings about the pressure to win; it may be more important just to be with his buddies. On the other hand, the child may be the competitive type who is frustrated by teammates who don't share his thirst for the sport. He should be encouraged to tolerate their laissez-faire approach while concentrating on improving his own skills.

Many times the child's opinions of his coach are reflected in his reactions to the sport, so the parents should try to find out what his feelings are about the coach. Does he like him? Does he feel comfortable playing for him? Or is the coach an intimidator? Does he terrify everybody on the team or just the players who aren't starting? Does he try to give attention to every player at practice, or is he really just concerned with the starting team?

Communicating athletically is not a one-way street. It's important that the parents express their opinions and make their needs known. But this should not be used as a coercive measure with the child. The father, for instance, can place his feelings out in the open by admitting, "Jeez, I really wish you would stay with football for one season. I'd like you to stick with it until the end. I feel it would be good for you and I think you would get a lot out of the sport if you gave it a chance. But if you want to quit, I can understand. I know what you're going through." In an open family like this, the child knows that he's not being compelled to follow his father's wishes. But if he knows how important football is to his father and he's sort of lukewarm, then he might think, "What the heck, I'll hang in there and do the best I can."

A healthy example of this perspective was provided by a father I knew who was once an outstanding pro football lineman. He dreamed that his son would play the same position, but he was also objective. He encouraged his son to participate in sports, but he let him know that he could play whatever sport he wanted and that he would support him. The son finally decided that he didn't like football, that he would rather devote himself to wrestling, a sport in which his father had never excelled. The son thus stayed in sports but he chose his own course, and the father could deal with the decision rationally, even though I could see that he was torn inside. "You know, I really wanted him to be a lineman," he told me, "but he'll be happier as a wrestler."

Everybody involved will gain from a family environment where questioning and discussion are accepted from an early age, by the parents as well as the children. In fact, athletic participation that takes place in a positive environment such as this can provide a medium for more effective child rearing. Long, warm conversations with the child who is involved in sports can provide strong moral support at a critical period in the child's development. This in turn can help build a tight-knit family that communicates openly in other important areas such as social development, dating, and schoolwork.

The Parental Model

Parents may condemn violence and abusive language and talk earnestly about such virtues as sportsmanship, cooperation, emotional control, and respect for authority, but, as the truism goes, children don't listen to what we say, they model what we do. And just as many professional athletes can communicate a destructive model, so parents must examine their actions in front of their children. They may, for instance, be exhibiting the same behavior under stress that their children display. The parents who shout and scream when things don't go their way at home are often the parents who are embarrassed and dismayed when their child flings his bat and kicks the dirt after striking out.

Other parents can be perfectly civilized around home, but they discard any concept of decorum and good-natured behavior when they watch their children compete. Having a child in Little League, in fact, seems to give parents a license to harangue the umpires, coaches, opposing players, and even their own child—all in behalf of building character. Witness the reaction of a 14-year-old boy who volunteered to umpire a Little League game in St. Paul, Minnesota. At one point the language and abusiveness got so bad, the boy said later: "I didn't know whether to throw out two mothers or the coach."

I remember one of the most painful incidents I've ever witnessed in Little League. Bobby was a terrific ballplayer—he could pitch, he could hit, and he could run—but his parents were really pushing him hard; they wanted him to be the best

player in the league. At the end of the second year in Little
League, Bobby pitched in the play-offs. Late in the game the
score was tied and he was at bat with two runners on base and
two outs. You could just see him dying to hit that ball, to drive
in the runs, because he would then shut the other team out and
win the game.

He was too eager, however. He swung at a bad pitch and
rapped the ball back to the pitcher, who threw to first for the
easy out. Bobby was seething as he ran towards first, as if his
whole world had fallen apart. In futility he went out of the
base path and knocked over the first baseman, trying to jar the
ball loose. Not only was he called out but he was thrown out of
the game. Tears were streaming down his face as he walked
towards the dugout, when suddenly his mother came storming
out of the stands. She marched up to him and belted him across
the head, and then began reprimanding him for what he had
just done.

Too bad the mother couldn't have been thrown out of the
park by a league-appointed vice-president in charge of temper
tantrums and foul language, who would roam through the
stands clearing out parents who clearly had their emotions and
priorities all scrambled up. Unfortunately, even that wouldn't
help their children when they got home. Many parents suffer
the same frustrations exhibited by Bobby's mother, except that
they don't leave the stands to hit their child. They usually wait
until they get home, and then if they don't hit him, they give
him a verbal working over.

On other occasions, the young athlete is not only influenced
by the behavior of his parents, but is also deeply embarrassed. I
knew of one situation, for example, where the father would sit
directly behind the team bench at the high school basketball
game. He had a bullhorn voice and would heap "advice" on his
boy, the other players, and the coach throughout the game.
The son was horribly ashamed of his father but was so
browbeaten that he couldn't say "Dad, you're causing me a lot
of grief." Finally, though, he got up enough courage to go to

the coach and at least apologize for his father's loudness. In some families the child is relieved when the parents don't show up for the game; when they are in the stands he feels that he's being judged on every play, or he's embarrassed when they try to talk to him during the game. I've even known of fathers who told the coach in front of the whole team that their son should be starting.

Problems such as these are unlikely to occur in a family where communication has been established and parents encourage feedback from their youngsters by asking questions such as "How do you feel about the way we're reacting?" In such families, the children invariably *want* their parents to watch them compete and to be around afterwards to enjoy the victory or to offer support in defeat. This gives the parents a chance to share even more of a common ground with their children.

If the parents can't show up for a game or a swim meet, they should explain the reasons to their youngsters. Otherwise he (or she) may feel that his parents don't care or are punishing him in some way, especially if there have been arguments over his participation.

Oftentimes the parents are not even aware of the behavior they are actually promoting. If their child's team has just lost, for instance, they might try to prop up his spirits by alibiing for the defeat—cursing the umpire, calling the coach a rotten fink, or criticizing the center fielder for his two errors. But that's not providing the child with a very healthy model for handling defeat. Furthermore, when the parents are critical of another player, the child can only empathize from being in that same position, and will feel that he, too, is receiving a critical reviewing during the game.

Similarly, the child's dissatisfaction with the coach may actually stem from some subtle communication by the parents. Every time the father watches football on television, he may call the coach stupid for using the wrong strategy—"How could he be so dumb to do that?" If this is a continual outburst every week, the message being given to the child is that coaches don't know what they're doing and father is really smarter, even though he's a floor manager at Dingle's Hardware. Thus the child can enter a sport like football with an underlying suspicion about coaches simply because this was the model presented by his father. The father may be totally unaware of what he has done. He may not even think that way about his son's coach. But the doubts and worries have been planted in the child's mind.

Parents should also be aware of the influence they can have on their youngsters when they take them to an athletic competition. If it's a team sport, every game automatically has good guys (the home team, in most cases) and bad guys (the visitors). But the true sports fan will root for his team while applauding the great plays on both sides. Furthermore, instead of belittling the home team when it loses, and being bitter and sarcastic, the parents who can respect the visitors—"Boy, that's a terrific team"—will convey a healthy response to their children.

Writer Clayton Riley discussed this distortion of competitive values in *Ms.* magazine, when contrasting the approach to sports by whites and blacks:

"Victory is primary to whites, *style* is to blacks," he wrote. "Winning is all any white ballplayer I've ever known is interested in. *How,* or the way victory looks, is insignificant."

He talked about O. J. Simpson, pro football's greatest running back, and how Simpson's "astonishing control of his body" was overlooked by many white fans because his team, the Buffalo Bills, were losers his first five years in the pros. Riley then quoted a friend, in summing up the whole question: "White boys only want to know what the final score was; they're only interested in the results. Brothers want to know what happened in the game, like, 'Did O. J. *dance?*' "

Competition within the Family

The child's competitive instincts will be honed from an early age by the nature of play and competition within his family. Once again the parents are the models. They set the pace and the approach to games in which the whole family participates, whether it's monopoly and checkers or volleyball and softball. Some parents communicate a fierceness of competition, turning fun and games into a life-and-death situation where everyone is expected to go all out to win. Instead of playing games primarily for relaxation and enjoyment, these parents (or one parent) gloat when they win and rub it in on the losers. This becomes a destructive model for the child, who looks forward to beating his parents in retaliation. One of the signs that a family is overdoing things is when everything becomes competitive: who eats dinner fastest, who does best in school, who has the cleanest pajamas, who can stay in the swimming pool longest. Life is a constant saturation of competition, and it's deadly if there's no support from the parents for doing one's best, at one's own pace.

Fortunately, in a society that is already producing too many competitive types, some parents nurture a cooperative approach to games involving children. They play games the children want to play, they make sure the sides are equal, they don't make a big fuss over who won and who lost, and they alter the rules to provide more enjoyment.

Though winning is the intent of every game, the idea should be for people—children as well as adults—to have fun along the way. Thus, mature parents never let themselves win every game. The child needs to learn *how* to lose, but to lose all the time is no fun and will only discourage him. Some parents, however, go overboard and purposely let their children win every time. That might be fine when they're very young, but as they get older there's sometimes a resentment that the parents don't try to win; children are not easily fooled and can be quick to suspect that the parent is letting them win. To even things up, the parents might take a handicap, especially in a sport like golf or tennis, and as the child's skill increases, the parents can decrease the handicap—until one day, of course, they are pleading for it.

The mature view of competition is to be able to have fun and enjoy playing under some sort of pressure. One thing a father can do when playing with his youngster is to set up a pressure situation and try to let him have success. They might play miniature basketball, for instance, and the father might say, "Alright, there are ten seconds left in the game. The next one who sinks it wins." It sounds artificial and it sounds like a bad scene. But what the father does is manage to come close but miss, and then the child gets the ball, or he lets the child take the first shot. If the child makes the basket, he has success in beating his father and his father sanctions it; nobody is threatened and both of them feel good.

It should be clearly understood, however, that the father is intentionally trying to help the child prepare for competition, and the child is young enough (under ten) so that there is enjoyment and a certain excitement about it. Furthermore, the child is not being evaluated on whether or not he makes the shot. If he doesn't make it, the father simply encourages him for his effort—"Nice shot, good try." He doesn't force the child to keep shooting until he sinks one. To do that is to destroy the child's willingness to compete under any pressure —to put his ego on the line, as opposed to developing a healthy competitive spirit where the child wants to test his limits and capabilities. The child should learn what competition and pressure are about—*in a supportive environment.* To plunge him immediately into a "sink it or else" situation is to ask for trouble.

I also think the parent can train his youngster to be tough and to enjoy it at the same time, without being cruel. If the father's aim is to have his son "become a man," the two of them can put on boxing gloves. The father lets the boy get his slugs in and he gives a few punches back, but nobody gets hurt. The boy learns to defend himself, he gets a chance to give his father a few licks, and he begins to understand what it's like to be tough. Yet the two of them are having fun; it's something they're doing together, and the child doesn't have to win or lose.

It must be remembered that all of this training is done with an educational intent. Winning isn't the important thing. The important thing is learning to cope maturely with an environment that is already competitive. To face this environment with a sense of confidence and a feeling of enjoyment will mean long-range benefits for the child, far beyond the fleeting effect of winning.

10

The Superstar:
A Curse or a Blessing?

THE FOCUS in this book thus far has been the average little athletes—their problems, their fears, their joys at achieving a measure of success in sports. But what about that handful of budding superstars in every league and every sport who find themselves swept up in a sometimes rewarding, oftentimes frustrating, dilemma? On the one hand they are singled out for early adulation and special treatment because of their talent and the success that it breeds. But meanwhile they are trapped by the reactions and assumptions of the adult world around them. Their physical skills may develop rapidly, but psychologically they can be undermined, like a little boy's carefully nurtured watermelon, which grows large and green, only to be eaten from underneath by an unsuspecting gopher.

This chapter will explore the young superstar from several viewpoints: the problems brought about by society's fascination with the athlete who has "potential"; the crucial role played by the parents; the funnel effect of high-level competitive sports; and some thoughts about families where child rearing is directed towards a college scholarship, a professional career, or the Olympics.

Society's Influences

The term *super* has become a sports phenomenon in the last ten or fifteen years. There are super teams, Super Bowls, superstars, and, to paraphrase a former vice-president, supercilious superjerks masquerading as sports heroes. On the professional level there's nothing more exciting, nothing more idolized than the athlete who is cast as a superstar. It is something that every athlete and his accountant dream about.

This concept of the superstar, however, like other myths in sports, has been barnacled with false assumptions. Foremost among these is the belief that since the superstar has physical talent, he automatically has other positive qualities as well, such as good looks, health, money, personality, and a wholesome, benevolent outlook on life. We assume that the superstar has everything, that he is happy and secure in his self-esteem, when in many cases he is searching desperately for that elusive happiness, a sense of contentment. If he's a superstar, he must now strive to become a Hall of Famer.

The tragedy is that the same kind of grandiosity prevails and the same assumptions are made by parents and coaches at the Pop Warner-Little League level. Everybody assumes that the little superstar, age eleven or twelve, or even younger, will be mature, cool under pressure, kind, considerate, lovable—the Boy Scout oath brought to life. But he's still just a little kid—with talent—and we should view him as simply that. Instead, when a child is recognized as having the potential for athletic greatness, a series of events begin to take place that shape his (or her) life and may undermine his emotional development.

He begins to establish a reputation and to be recognized by other people for his ability. It starts with people telling him that he is a good player. That leads to "You're a great player!"

And from there to "We're going to win with you!" Soon he begins to realize that he is important to the community, maybe even a focus of attention in the media. (In many towns this can happen at the high school level, but in Taiwan the nationwide adulation is for their Little League heroes.) By word and by deed the young superstar is reminded repeatedly that he can do no wrong. Members of his peer group envy him, younger children imitate and emulate him—he becomes a hero in other people's eyes. If he does not have the emotional stability to put himself into proper perspective, he begins to believe that he deserves the adulation.

The potential superstar is treated in such a way that excuses are made for his errors. People are so worried about his temperament that they fail to correct him; they compensate for him and excuse him from mundane activities for fear that he will become unhappy and not perform up to par. By pampering him, paving his way, taking care of his needs, and providing special privileges, people help perpetuate any immaturity that may be there. The athlete begins to think that people will give him these things all his life and he begins to expect them—"the world owes me a living." His vision of reality becomes completely distorted.

The athlete may soon realize that he has a great deal of power and will begin to use his performances as a tool. If his needs are taken care of, he performs well. But if he feels neglected or not taken care of in the manner he thinks he deserves, he may perform poorly. This becomes his greatest weapon, and more often than not he ends up getting his way or is placated by those in charge.

In exchange for these perquisites of stardom, undue pressure is often placed on the young superstar before he is capable of handling it. If he performs well, people begin to expect that he will perform well all the time. When he doesn't, they are disappointed. If the athlete sees the disappointment and is immature, he may begin to blame many other things for the failure, such as officials, field conditions, poor coaching, teammates, and so on. Part of maturity is admitting one's mistakes and adjusting to them. If people help the superstar excuse himself for making errors, they are really helping him learn to evade reality.

The young superstar—even the good player who is bigger than his teammates—must deal with the assumption held by some adults that because he is so much in command in athletics, he is well adjusted in social situations and does not have the same emotional needs as the other members of his peer group. Realistically, of course, he's not further developed *psychologically* than most of his teammates. He may even be more shy and may need more help than others his age. If adults fail to provide this help and the necessary understanding, but continue to protect him, feed his dependency needs, and never permit him to grow, then from a psychological viewpoint he becomes a cripple, unable to take care of himself, always expecting handouts from others. When he moves to the next level of competition, he may be inadequate in terms of facing it from a personality standpoint. Because of his ability, he is shoved into ever-increasing pressure and higher levels of competition before he has had the opportunity to "practice maturity." If he fails, he may begin to show more and more immature behavior. Failure may cause him to feel extremely depressed and even account for a complete loss of interest in the sport. The athlete who punishes himself for not living up to expectations may find the pressure so severe that he quits athletics rather than take the pain and the disappointment. If, however, the athlete experiences success despite these new pressures, it may serve only to establish his feelings of importance and to distort his perspective even more.

Ultimately, however, the biggest problems to be faced by a budding superstar will lie with his parents. Some parents, who will never be known for making any contribution in their life, may begin to treat their son's glory as their own. They will brag about him to their friends and keep his trophies prominently displayed in the living room. When this happens, the child is looked after, cared for, and loved—but only if he performs, or more properly, only *because* he performs. If he begins to fail, or begins to develop interests in other directions, it's a genuine threat to the parents.

The Role of the Parents

Parents who have a potential superstar should realize one basic truth: the child may have great talent, but they can make or break him emotionally. They are the ones most responsible for the delicate job of counterbalancing the pressures that their child will face from his teammates, his coaches, his public, and himself. It may sound obvious and trite, but love must be shown for the *individual,* not for what that individual is capable of doing in athletics. Love and acceptance are what the child wants, but too often what he gets is love with conditions. If the parents love the child only because he is a first stringer, a winner, a hero, then the day will come when he will run out of first teams, victories, and heroics, and find he is alone. It is tough enough to find that out when you are 20 or 30 or 35 years of age. It is deadly, psychologically, to discover it at age 12 or 13.

Another problem that can arise in the family with a young superstar was brought out one night at a meeting of Little League parents and coaches in San Jose. One father in the audience asked me, "What do you do with a son who's an outstanding ball player but he's obnoxious? He thinks baseball is everything." Everybody broke into laughter, appreciating the man's frustration, although I'm afraid some of them would have been willing to swap their well-adjusted, bench-warming son for the chance to raise a superstar (at least on game days).

I told the father, "One thing you could do is talk to your son about reality. Help him put sports in perspective and get him to realize that baseball is not making monumental contributions to mankind. Sports is entertainment, and when entertainment becomes the central feature in a person's life, one has to question his or her values." I went on to say that when society overemphasizes the value of sports, it's only natural that the athletes—from Pop Warner to the National Football League—think they're making a greater contribution than they are. They should be reminded that sports can give them something, but the only thing they can give the sport is their talent.

I always urge parents not to let their child develop a distorted picture of himself and his importance to the team. Otherwise he could begin to feel superior in other areas—to act holier-than-thou on the playground, in the classroom, and even around the house. He'll begin to feel that he has something due him because of his athletic skill. As Thomas Johnson, the San Diego child psychologist, points out: "The superstar should be told quietly and shown by parental actions that he has no special privileges simply because he's an outstanding athlete; this doesn't excuse him not doing his homework." Even on his own team it will be easy for others to resent him and his ability; if he is immature and arrogant in return, he will provide a fertile soil for these hostile feelings to grow. For example, at critical times during a game, especially in a sport like basketball, he may attempt to take over completely and do it all by himself. He does not wish to identify with the rest of the team because he sees them as losers. Some superstars will even say openly, "I'm playing on a lousy team. I can't do it all."

One way to keep the athlete's accomplishments and notoriety in perspective is to encourage him to help some of the other players on the team, but not in a condescending manner. Prod him to lead by example rather than always flaunting his ability; ask him to help the youngster with all thumbs rather than make fun of him. Even in the preadolescent years the budding superstar will have younger players who admire him. Thus his parents could remind him, "You know, little Fenwick thinks a lot of you. Maybe you could spend a little time with him at practice and try to help him instead of putting him down. He thinks you're somebody special, but when you laugh at his errors, that hurts his feelings."

The parents should not only help their child keep a level head when he is a hero, but should also help him learn to recognize failure and not try to deny it. He must be taught to face life realistically. The emphasis should be that when something goes wrong, accept the blame and do something about it—work harder, hustle, concentrate, learn to relax, etc. The more there is a tendency by the child to blame others and not accept responsibility, the more he's going to end up saying, "Well, it wasn't my fault. It was the field's fault. The grass was wet and I kept slipping." Here is where the parents very clearly need to be the model. Instead of ripping into the poor play of other players in order to make his son feel better, the father should empathize with someone who hasn't done well or shift the emphasis to his son's play. Perhaps the son contributed to the team's problems with his own mistakes. If he repeatedly hears excuses from his parents or coaches—"That damn umpire was terrible. . . . Boy, your guards killed you with all those turnovers"—the child may learn to think he can escape responsibility simply by finding the proper scapegoat. One way to develop a con man, in fact, is to convince him that when something goes wrong, it is not his fault.

A positive example of parental involvement was supplied by Milwaukee shortstop Robin Yount, who was a major-league starter at the age of eighteen. Yount said he learned to play ball in the family backyard with his father and that his father prodded and taught him, but never pushed: "When I'd strike out a few times in a game, Dad wouldn't say anything, but just volunteer to pitch batting practice to me. We'd hang a tarp as a backstop and I could swing as hard as I wanted to because the ball would sail into a walnut orchard and come right back down to the yard."

Some parents make a crucial mistake in trying to help their youngster maintain a perspective on success and fame. Instead of praising the child's effort after a strong performance, they will belittle or ignore what he did right simply because they don't want him to "get a big head"; for instance, the father who says of his superstar son: "He doesn't need to hear from me—he knows how good he is." This is unfair to the child. He worked hard, he came through under pressure, he did what was asked of him. For his parents now to give only grudging approval or to start criticizing minor flaws in his performance is to place him in a vicious cycle that will only lead to more acting out on his part in a desperate effort to gain his parents' goodwill.

The key is objectivity. It's damaging for everyone concerned when the parents gloat endlessly over their child's athletic accomplishments, especially when other parents are around who have less talented children.

In addition to the difficulties of handling fame—and defeat—the talented youngster who seems determined to devote his teenage years to acquiring an athletic scholarship or a pro contract needs to be warned that the problems he will face are different from the problems faced by most athletes. First, a number of people will use him and try to live vicariously through him. Second, he will find that everybody wants to be his friend and to be around him as much as possible. This may seem nice at first, but eventually it can wear away his patience and tolerance. If he is the kind of person who cannot say no and set limits, he might experience considerable pain and loss of identity. Third, everyone wants to possess him. Some use him to fulfill their personal needs or to make money; girls seek a form of recognition and a feeling of importance through him. And fourth, one of the prerequisites of handling athletic success is the ability to live with fan rejection. The *f* in *fan* stands for fickle. They love you today—but you had better win tomorrow. The youngster won't always be a "winner," and so he must learn to tolerate unfair and unreasonable fan reaction. In fact, even when he is winning, his fans can grow restless if he doesn't perform to an expected level of excellence: their greed for greater and greater exploits knows no limit. "We keep projecting our fantasies on sports figures, then burdening them with our disappointments when they fail," wrote Jon Carroll in an article on Chris Evert. "To retain our respect, they must be paragons of skill, charm and enlightened thinking." If the superstar, or any athlete for that matter, lets these expectations interfere with his performance, he's in serious trouble.

Parents with a superstar daughter in the family must not only help her maintain a perspective on life, they must help her contend with the social and psychological pressures that exist in a society where boys are pushed into an athletic role early while girls are frightened off. As hurdler Patty Johnson points out, "It's natural for an athlete, boy or girl, to desire to excel. Yet the athletic girl is regarded as a tomboy and, therefore, unfeminine." Even with today's lessening stereotypes of the female athlete, the girl with talent must still overcome pressures from parents, other adults, and even peers *not* to become a full-fledged, year-round athlete—except, of course, in Olympic sports like swimming, diving, gymnastics, and figure skating. Great as a girl's desire might be to excel in sports, the feeling still persists that the time will come when she has to sacrifice either her athletic ability or her femininity. In many families, if she persists in trying to be an athlete while her parents simply want her to be a daughter, she can suffer through a real identity crisis.

The Funnel Effect

The professional sports enterprise is so highly visible—with all that money, all those new leagues, and all that public notoriety—that the outstanding young athlete is led to believe he, too, can reach the limelight if he is dedicated and works hard. Yet few people stop to think just how few openings there are in a profession that is only half as big as canned soup, in economic terms. To devote one's life to attaining that goal is like investing all your money in one stock.

In 1975, there were six major team sports (football, basketball, hockey, baseball, tennis, and soccer) and approximately 135 teams, with no more than 3,500 players on active playing rosters. Out of these, no more than 1,740 could be classed as starters. More specifically, the Department of Labor released a study which showed the diminishing returns in baseball. Of the millions of boys who play Little League, about 400,000 will eventually play high school baseball, about 25,000 will go on to play college ball, and about 100 will make it into the major leagues. And just a handful of those will have a career that lasts as long as seven years. In pro football, even those who survive the rigorous weeding-out process (one estimate is that pro football players are the best 1/10,000th of 1 percent of those exposed to the game) can anticipate a career that averages only five years. Basketball figures show that in 1974 there were 200,000 high school seniors and 5,700 college seniors playing the game, of which 211 players were drafted by the pros and 55 were signed.

Unfortunately, we're not preparing our athletes for these realities. There is a continual buildup but seldom the precaution of a great letdown, as parents and coaches nurture the child's (and their own) grandiose dreams that he's going to be the one to make it. This doesn't mean that parents should keep telling their child, "You're never going to make it. That's a foolish goal." After all, a single-minded dedication and inner self-confidence are commonalities of most champions. What the youngster does need, however, if he is determined to carve out a career in sports, is for his parents to provide a realistic appraisal of the frightening odds that are working against him, and the unexpected reversals that can ambush his hopes before they are fulfilled. The youngster needs to be encouraged to develop confidence and interests in other areas besides sports. If sports become the sole aspect of his life, he can easily be cut off from other influences that could contribute to his growth as a person. For example, swimmers are training or competing nearly every day, all year round. They begin to narrow their lives when they are ten or eleven, at a crucial period of personal development and self-awareness. Their parents are, in essence, encouraging them to believe that life revolves around swimming, which is unfair to the child.

Vic Braden, the veteran tennis coach, says: "I have parents come and tell me, 'Vic, please get my kid to give up basketball. It's going to spoil his tennis game.' I tell them, 'I don't think any sport or any activity should own a monopoly on a child's life.' " Instead of specializing in one sport, a talented youngster should be encouraged to "follow the seasons" from sport to sport. He will develop more strength and flexibility as an all-around athlete, he will keep a fresh perspective on each sport, and he will know that he has not invested all of his hopes in just one basket.

The athlete who places his future in one sport has to step back periodically and think, "What if something happens to me? What if I don't make it in football?" He needs to be prepared for setbacks along the way—the trauma of a knee injury that steals his speed and agility, or the coach or manager who finally says, "Kid, you're not going to make it. This is as far as you go."

It is difficult to think of another profession where the opportunity for advancement often gets cut off at the peak of an individual's career. Overnight the athlete can be stripped of a sport and a life-style that brought him pleasure and recognition for many years. Let us take an athlete in high school who is told that he has the potential for greatness but to develop it he must work long and hard, to the exclusion of everything but the necessary schoolwork. He continues to participate in college and then finds that he does not have the necessary skills to make it on a professional level. He may be an outstanding athlete, but because he's too short or too small his name is rejected by scouting computers. Where does he turn? By this time he has become some kind of expert in his field. He did as he was told—he dedicated his life to the sport—only to find that when he didn't make it he was left with four choices in relation to the sport: to flounder in semipro or amateur ball for years and end up with nothing; to be an official or some other peripheral part of athletics; to complete college as a physical education major with the hope of becoming a P.E. instructor or coach; or to become a well-informed spectator who receives little of the old satisfaction he knew as a participant. Some athletes are so unprepared for the abrupt end of their career that they are often unable to cope with life outside the pool, the gym, or the athletic field—whether it involves handling their money or relationships with other people—once they're an ex-athlete and out of the limelight.

Darrell Royal, the University of Texas football coach, thinks the best thing that can happen to some of his former players is to get dumped by the pro teams. "I often call my players who get cut and congratulate them," he said. "I'm really glad when they get this pro football business out of their system." He noted that marginal players who make the pro ranks "barely hang on for six or seven years," then learn when they retire that they have neither financial security nor stability. "They find themselves six or seven years older without a job."

"I'd like to see our boys with something on the ball channel their intelligence elsewhere," Royal continued. "A few players will be in the high money bracket and the rest will never get very much. I'm not knocking professional athletics, but it all depends on the individual."

The black athlete is the most tragic victim of the funnel effect. Millions of talented black youngsters are playing sports across the country, but professional sports can absorb only so many; in a sport like basketball the bottleneck is forcing blacks to beat out other blacks just to make the team, or the starting lineup. Sociologist Dr. Harry Edwards, who was at the forefront of the black athletes revolt in the late 1960s, views organized sports as "a trap leading nowhere for most black youngsters, and the failure, the disillusionment, leads to social unrest and subsequent crime." He argues that instead of American society demanding that "black youth strive first and foremost to be the world's great athletes," there has to be "the same encouragement and drive for black kids to want to become doctors, scientists, politicians, and lawyers."

Other black educators, such as New York University's Dr. Roscoe C. Brown, Jr., are angered by "the disproportionate amount of energy spent in the ghetto developing sport skills." He charges that most blacks find neither social mobility, educational fulfillment, or financial success through what he calls "the mirage" of sports recruiting. Most of those black athletes who are rejected by the sports system "are left without the skills needed for servicing or enriching the community, and that's the ripoff."

Healthy Competition or Child Abuse

The child who displays athletic talent at an early age or the child with parents who dream that their offspring will one day be a successful athlete can generally anticipate that he (or she) will be given the "opportunity" to develop that talent and the hopes of the parents. At first it may mean a small amount of practice after school. But if the sport is a pursuit such as age-group swimming, tennis, gymnastics, or figure skating, the child may soon be training three or four hours every day, in addition to going to school and trying to cope with homework and the normal problems of growing up.

One reason for this hard, early push in sports is the knowledge that this has been the route for countless champions. For example, thousands of little swimmers get up at five o'clock every morning to freeze their tails off, hoping they'll go to the Olympics, and they'll never make it. They will put in thousands of hours of useless energy, in a sport they don't even like. But their mothers will say, "Mark Spitz did it."

Parents in other individual sports have their own current examples of how early obsession leads to success, such as Jimmy Connors, Chris Evert, Cathy Rigby, and Janet Lynn.

A second motivation is the realization and fear that our international Olympic rivals like Russia and East Germany, not to mention the Canadian hockey leagues, are up to the same tricks. The latest gambit by the Russians is a special factory-sponsored school in Soviet Central Asia where six- and seven-year-old children are carefully tested for swimming potential. They are given 36 free lessons and then timed at 25 meters. Six months later they are tested again and those showing the most potential (1 out of 10, or about 125 a year) are placed in a special swimming program featuring an Olympic-sized pool and 12 full-time and about 30 part-time coaches. With the Americans as their model and their target, these children train twice a day, six days a week as part of their regular curriculum. (Meanwhile, one powerful Russian sports club has announced that it will open a boarding school for future hockey players, starting at age eight and will build them an indoor rink. But are the youth sports leaders of this country any less obsessed with building future champions? We have little ice hockey factories in cities everywhere trying to produce American-bred hockey heroes who can take over the professional game. "It should take us until 1980 to catch the Canadians," boasted one Los Angeles junior hockey official. "We have an advantage over Canada: ice the year round. They have no indoor rinks. Our season starts in September and ends in March, and from March to September we have hockey schools and clinics to keep our ice time. Otherwise the figure skaters take over.")

Third, there are the insatiable, Spartan demands required by nearly every sport if one hopes to acquire the expertise and conditioning not only to reach the national-international level of competition, but simply to remain competitive in one's own city or town. We're organizing our team and individual sports so well, right down to the five-and six-year olds, that many parents are led to believe that their child will fall hopelessly behind youngsters his own age if he's not out there competing as soon as the rules, or coach, allows.

Let's look at swimming, where the demands of the sport (and thus of the coach, the parents, and the child) result in a grinding, year-round regimen calling for two-a-day workouts, extreme self-discipline, and an ability to withstand pain while laboring lap after lap in heavily clorinated water. "It's like a mileage race to nowhere," said the mother of one Los Angeles swimmer. Swimmers take pride in having the mental toughness to endure this almost daily suffering, then come back the next morning when it is still dark and take the punishment all over again. The implicit understanding with the sport seems to be that surviving this agony will somehow make the swimmer a stronger, better person. Perhaps it does, but at what cost?

Objectively speaking, one has seriously to question the claims that swimming is a healthily adjusted sport. I feel that it requires a neurotic approach to competition and to living one's life. The sport is a complete preoccupation in which nearly every other aspect of normal living is eliminated. Even down to the food they eat, top swimmers have to think: "Will it be good for my swimming?" Once a youngster makes a commitment to the sport, she (or he) is forced to narrow her experiences and her behavior. She loses social interaction away from the pool and the ability to develop social graces; dating is something you do after you retire. Of the thousands of things she could be doing, all she knows about is swimming. Not only that: the longer she stays in swimming, and the better she becomes, the more her obsession must grow to meet the ever-increasing competitive pressures.

But why? What is the payoff? My associate, Bruce Ogilvie, whose daughter swam for the famed Santa Clara Swim Club, once observed: "I don't know of any other sport that has so many signs of success—the medals, ribbons, trophies, age-group records. The kids learn habits that are greatly reinforced. It's truly incredible. My daughter went through this for George Haines and once she got hooked on making the national team, to swim internationally, she was swimming three times a day, two hours at a clip. There's no way you could ask a child to do that. It scares you. But boy, that goal held out there as a possibility is really something."

Shirley Babashoff, one of the world's leading swimmers, typifies the attitude of those who are successful in the sport. She started swimming competitively at age nine; by the time she was sixteen, a year AFTER she won a gold medal in the Munich Olympics, her weekday schedule looked like this: awake at 4:30 A.M., workouts from 5:30 to 7:00 A.M., school at 9:30 A.M., home and nap at 1:30 P.M., dinner at 3:30 P.M., workouts again from 4:30 P.M. to 7:30 P.M., home at 8:15 P.M., a snack and then to bed. On weekends she would train five hours a day. Asked if she felt that complete attention to swimming was keeping her from enjoying life, she replied: "How can you say you can't live when you can win a gold medal in the end and meet new people from all the different countries? It all kind of makes up for what you've lost—and more."

One mistake people make is to judge swimming from Babashoff's perspective; there were 140,000 competitive swimmers in the United States in 1974, but only a handful of those would ever have the opportunity to win an Olympic medal or make foreign friends. Meanwhile, most swimmers retire from the sport in their mid-teens, frazzled by the long hours of training and the pressure of competition. When former Olympic star Debbie Meyer looked back on her career, in coach Sherm Chavoor's book *The Fifty Meter Jungle*, the agony of trying to remain competitive still scarred her memory:

I had to learn to live with pain. I often wanted to jump out of the pool and choke Sherm. He treated us like mechanical robots but it was the only way to win.

You have no idea what the pain is. As you swim it starts in the legs. First they feel numb and itch from lack of oxygen. Then the numbness turns into a searing ache. It spreads through the legs into the midsection, and then into the lungs.

Every breath becomes torture. Then the pain moves into the arms and you almost wish they'd drop off. At the age of 20 the pain wasn't worth it anymore—and I quit.

Every semester I have students come up after a class to tell me, "You know, I just don't like to swim anymore. I started swimming when I was six and when I was twelve I was burned out." Not only that; former swimmers often resent their parents or their coach because they feel they were cheated out of childhood and were never able to experience the normal course of growing up that others had. Donna de Varona, a beautiful swimming heroine of the early 1960s, admits she had everything—and yet, "I felt like such a nobody. I got dates in high school because I was Donna de Varona, the swimmer, not because I was me." Penn State gymnast Karen Schuckman, who was told she had Olympic potential when she was ten, recalled in *Sports Illustrated*: "My first boyfriend was 23. I was 15. I looked at my friends in school and saw what they were doing and realized what a warped social life I had. As a young kid you don't understand what's happening, how you got there, the route you took. You know only that you started to do it because it was fun and then you had a guide [a coach] who led you and you just followed."

Whether we admit it or not, we have developed an acceptable form of physical child abuse in sports where children must train two times a day or in a single stretch of three to four hours. We get our children up before dawn and drive them to the swimming pool or ice rink, where they work for two hours before school. We classify it as fun—"It's alright, it's athletics"—but you certainly don't see many children enjoying themselves. Not to mention their bleary-eyed parents. Sadly, most of the children involved in this training grind do not have the talent or the genes to become an eventual winner let alone a Debbie Meyer or Mark Spitz, and yet they are expected to devote the same amount of time as the stars in the club. We treat all of them as if they were eager professionals, yet they receive none of the benefits of being a professional. They don't get the notoriety, they aren't allowed a voice, and they aren't even getting paid. We assume that the pay will be winning, or a mantel with medals and trophies, or trips to out-of-state competition. Yet once they taste success, the pressures simply increase; they must work even harder to keep winning and to strive for the top. If they are unsuccessful, however, in a highly charged competitive environment, where little support is given to those who fail, they lose all the way around.

Ultimately, the young athlete must have the final say on whether he plays a sport, and at what age, and with what dedication. The parents should offer their advice, their encouragement, and their involvement, but not an ultimatum. The child and his parents may in fact be working out their compulsions together. Yet the child must be the one to decide whether he simply wants to be with his friends, to eventually win a high school letter, to earn a college scholarship, or to strive for an ultimate athletic dream such as the Olympics or the pros. Reaching for such a goal is fine for those who have voluntarily selected this way of life, who feel it is their "thing," who know the odds against them, and who are more than willing to dedicate the time, the effort, and the pain in the attempt to reach the top.

It is a criminal act, however, to force a hard, competitive life on a reluctant child through overwhelming pressures by the family and community. Such coercion can only lead a child to feel he is trapped in a psychological concentration camp, where there is no alternative but to compete. Adults assume that the child has volunteered to be there and wants to be there because of the rewards the sport offers, notably the chance to win. But the child's viewpoint might be entirely different. All he knows is that he has to go out to practice every day and suffer. He has to drive himself to exhaustion and then come back and prove that he can do it again at the next workout. Given a *free* choice between the elusive rewards and being happy, he might very well say, "I'm giving it up. It's just not worth it any more."

If adults were placed in the same position of trying to cope with school, their sport, and growing up—all under intense pressure—most of them would scoff and quickly rebel: "Are you crazy?" But the child in this situation knows that if he tries to quit he will be punished by his parents, if not physically then mentally. They give him the illusion of freedom—"You can always quit if you want to"—only to try to talk him out of it if the situation arises. Another problem occurs when the coach uses the parents to encourage the child to "gut it out" or to work harder, without looking at the child's perspective. Then it becomes three adults against the child, who will simply be forced to stay in the sport. A quote by Shirley Babashoff is indicative of the subtle pressures that can exist. "I've always wanted to swim," she said, "but sometimes I've wanted to quit, too. My mom and Flip Darr [her former coach] are the ones who snap me out of it. They give me pep talks. They make excuses for me when I lose."

11

Injuries

PROPONENTS OF HIGHLY COMPETITIVE childhood sports argue that the danger of injury is overblown by a sensationalist press and by "tear-down" critics within the ranks of physicians, educators, and child psychologists. One difficulty in drawing appropriate attention to the injury risks in most sports at this level is the lack of specific research data regarding the incidence of injuries. Many preadolescent sports events are lucky to have a physician present, let alone someone researching injuries or writing about them in the newspaper. When specific evidence showing a clear injury pattern *does* surface, the tendency of those in charge of sports programs is to ignore the findings. For instance, in San Bernardino, California, in the late 1960s, Dr. Joel Adams studied comparative X rays of 162 baseball players between the ages of nine and fourteen; all 80 pitchers in the study, plus a few catchers, showed "some evidence of varying degree of reaction to the repetitious stress involving the growth line of the elbow joint of the throwing arm, depending on the amount of throwing."

The results led Adams to advocate important rule changes regarding the use of young pitchers, but they have been widely ignored in Little Leagues across the country.

Competitive sports for children pose physical dangers which should never be slighted by parents. For one thing, there's the risk of possible permanent damage to the child's growing body through injury of the epiphyses, or "growth lines," located at the ends of bones. The danger, doctors say, is not so much from the injury itself, which results from vigorous stress on the muscles and ligaments attached to the epiphyses, but from failure to recognize the stress and institute proper treatment. Secondly, adult supervision in our highly organized sports structure doesn't guarantee that proper safety precautions are being observed. Dr. James Nicholas, the prominent New York sports doctor, points out that knowledgeable treatment of athletic injuries rarely reaches below the collegiate and professional level. "Top-flight care is only in the province of several hundred high schools, many colleges, and most pro teams," he said, and many Little League-level events are played without a doctor present. Furthermore, the adults involved are too often caught up in the competitive aspects of the sport (i.e., winning) and are not always concerned first and foremost with the physical well-being of the youngsters involved. Robert Gans, a Beverly Hills doctor, warns against football coaches, for instance, who encourage their players to try to run off the field when they're hurt. "Why?" he asks. "It's a false sign of courage. If the player trots off or is helped off it could make the difference between a mild and a severe reaction, especially if he has a head injury."

This is another symptom of the play-in-pain syndrome which, as noted earlier, is a glorified element in professional, collegiate, and high school sports. Coaches love to praise the athlete who can play with a broken nose, cracked ribs, a temperature of 102, or a pulled muscle—"He's a real competitor"—and use him as the embodiment of team spirit. The tragedy is that this false sense of heroics is ingrained in many youngsters at an early age, by parents and coaches alike. The result can be seen in Pop Warner football practices, where the boy who is slow to get up during tackling exercises (he may have a bloody nose or have been knocked dizzy) is shamed out of showing his pain by a coach who stands there shouting, "Come on, come on, get up—show us you're a man! We don't want any sissies out here!" So the boy tries to "gut it out," convinced that his status in the eyes of his coach or his teammates is more important than his own protesting body. Some boys will downplay injuries or not report them rather than risk humiliation by the coach or their father. They are led to believe that to show pain is to show weakness as a person, that only girls cry when they are hurt. They may be afraid that they will lose their starting position if they miss a game or two because of injuries.

Another influence can be guilt. Young athletes often feel that they are somehow letting their parents down by getting injured. In an article on the U.S. figure skating championships in 1974, *Sports Illustrated* writer Jeanette Bruce commented: "Parents were inclined to attend only those competitions in which their darlings appeared. Spills in practice sessions, as tension grew, produced one hairline fracture, a strained tendon and a torn ligament. 'If your parents have sacrificed a lot,' one skater said, 'and you break something, you feel terrible. There goes your $5,000 axle.' "

Some parents will even risk long-range physical damage by, for instance, allowing a cortisone shot in their twelve-year-old's ailing knee so that he can play in Saturday's "important" game. One Houston pediatrician reported that parents have even called him to ask if their son could play baseball with a broken nose. Then there are the parents who refuse to accept "minor" injuries to their child. "Shake it off, it doesn't really hurt" is their on-the-spot evaluation, as if the child should be able to separate the pain from the injury. These parents feel it's a sign of weakness if the child complains about bumps and bruises and getting the wind knocked out of him; in order to learn what life is all about, they reason, he has to go through a certain amount of suffering. Other parents suspect that the child's complaint is a ploy to get out of practice, or that he is learning how to take the easy way out. In reality, what may be happening is that the child is trying to tell his parents that he really doesn't enjoy his particular sport. Secretly, he may even see injuries as a blessing, a way to ease out of the sport without simply quitting.

Says Dr. James Garrick, head of the division of sports medicine at the University of Washington: "We take the philosophy when dealing with pre-college-age youngsters that if they tell us they're injured and we are unable to document the injury, then this means one of two things: (a) we're not smart enough to find the injury or (b) they don't want to play. Either of these is a legitimate reason for not continuing participation. I am not aware of any young person whose character has been improved by forcing him to be involved in an activity—often with an appreciable risk of injury—that he was actively trying to avoid."

In view of the injury hazard that exists in competitive sports at all levels, parents should take the following precautions to see that their youngster plays in a safety-conscious environment. These steps can lessen the odds that their child will be hurt during a given season and can also help to ensure correct diagnosis, handling, and treatment should an injury occur.

1. Every child should receive a preparticipation physical exam and should not be allowed to play without a certificate of suitability. The exam doesn't have to be elaborate or sophisticated—a twelve-year-old hardly needs a stress ECG or a complete blood chemistry panel—but it should include baseline stability tests of knees and ankles, and the doctor should be aware of any previous injury to the musculoskeletal system or the central nervous system. If the examining physician is someone other than the family doctor or pediatrician, he should have a written medical history of the youngster. The athlete

can often forget—or conveniently overlook—past illnesses or operations. Dr. Joseph Torg, an expert on sports injuries, commented: "There are many things we simply can't pick up on examinations or we wouldn't pick up unless we had been tipped off. The child who has asthma on exertion, for example. Unless you take him out and stress him you are never going to know unless you hear it from someone else. He may be ashamed of it or he may intentionally not tell you."

Medical advances, fortunately, have made it possible for asthmatic and diabetic youngsters to compete in sports. However, if the doctor feels that *any* youngster is ill suited physically to play a contact sport, he should try to discuss the situation with the youngster and the parents. The doctor could perhaps encourage participation in an individual sport, or one where size or a lack of strength is not such a negative factor.

2. Any time the child reports pain or has obviously been injured, a checkup should be made, innocent as the injury may seem to the coach or parents. For example, the same blow that knocks the wind out can also rupture the spleen. And tears or fractures of the "growth line" in the ankles, knees, elbows, and spine can cause permanent damage to an immature skeleton if left undiagnosed or to "work themselves out." Youngsters should also be given a medical exam at the end of the season so that undetected or unreported injuries can be caught by the doctor.

3. Parents and coaches need to insist on protective equipment that is safe to use. Dr. James Garrick, one of the foremost advocates of meaningful reform in injury prevention, talked about the lack of serious attention being paid to this area: "We seem to be well informed about the healthy athlete and how he functions and about the seriously injured athlete and how he might be repaired. We are not so well informed about the task of keeping the healthy athlete from becoming an injured athlete." Unfortunately, he points out, "preventive medicine is not a saleable commodity. It's like safety. But we need to set standards for protective equipment." Garrick, who is currently

researching athletic injuries for the National Consumer Safety Products Commission, feels that on the preadolescent level, the parents and the coach (or his equipment manager) must be educated in respect to equipment selection, maintenance, and fitting to safety. Initial responsibility for equipment safety lies with the manufacturer, he says, but ultimately the burden rests heavily upon the adults who are involved in each sport. "The inherent degree of risk already existing in baseball, football and hockey can be increased by ill-fitting or maintained equipment resulting from a lack of awareness that such items as a loosely fitting batting helmet, a faulty shoulder pad or a missing knee pad can lead to injury."

4. The parents should determine whether there is proper medical supervision during competition as well as practices. Ideally, a physician should be present or easily available for all games and practice sessions, especially in sports like football, baseball, and hockey. Research has shown that as many injuries occur during football practice as during a game, yet prompt and adequate medical treatment at practices is a haphazard proposition at best and oftentimes simply nonexistent. There may not even be a telephone available for summoning help.

5. Concerned parents should learn what training the coach has in injury detection and treatment. In Garrick's opinion, "It's not realistic to think you'll get a doctor at every practice, so coaches have to become injury-recognizers. They need to be trained to recognize and diagnose injuries so that the child is not further injured by improper treatment."

6. The doctor must always have the final say when dealing with the injured youngster, the coach, and the parents. Without the doctor on his side, the youngster can be at the mercy of a coach or parents who have hard-nosed attitudes about pain and a little suffering. As Garrick points out: "Little children won't stand up to their coach. They'll do anything to please him; they live on praise. If the football coach tells an 8-year-old to 'get the hell back in there,' the boy will do what he says, even if he's hurting." Dr. Charles J. Frankel, professor

of orthopedics at the University of Virginia Medical School, urges physicians to stand up against a coach who wants an athlete to play when the physician knows he shouldn't: "You must have the understanding that the coach can't practice medicine and the doctor won't coach. If you don't have that arrangement, you've got a disaster plan."

The physician must stay emotionally aloof from the game and the team, especially if his own youngster is a member. He can't be so caught up in the team's success that he leaves an injured player in the game a little longer because the coach believes that "winning is the best medicine." Of course, the coach is not always the culprit; oftentimes the athlete himself, in order to get back in the game, will lie about his condition. So the doctor must act decisively, and always with the child's physical well-being foremost in mind. If there's any doubt about a youngster's condition, he should be pulled from the game, or taken out of competition if it's an individual sport. The player who has been shaken up may be able to play—"but don't take a chance," warns Joel Adams. "If he's alright, he can play in the next game. You can't treat kids the way you treat adults. You've got to give nature a chance to heal them." Occasionally the doctor is pressured by a coach or by parents to give cortisone shots to youngsters with gimpy knees or sore arms so they can play in the championship game. But as Dr. Robert Kerlan, medical director of the National Athletic Health Institute in Los Angeles, said: "With a little kid, you never take a chance. You never make a bruise feel better so he can play."

One danger in an individual sport like gymnastics or swimming, Adams points out, comes when a youngster shows real promise and the coach increases the training. He puts the youngster on "an Olympic Training Schedule," which can lead to injuries resulting from repetitive stress on the growth lines. The family or team doctor can often be caught in this situation between his concern for the child's welfare and the ambitions of the parents or the coach. Adams once treated a thirteen-year-old girl gymnast who was being pushed hard to become a success. "She had been training and competing since she was five years old and her shoulder joints were already creaking," he said. "When I told her she needed a period of complete rest and to stop competing, she was the happiest girl in the world. Finally there was someone official to tell her, 'Stop!' But her coach thought I was a stinker—I took away his future Olympic champion."

7. Every sport needs safety-minded game officials. If an athlete is slightly injured or badly shaken up, but is allowed to remain in the game by the coach, the officials should have the power to remove that athlete for a certain period of time. The player should not be allowed back in the game until he has been examined by a physician or a team trainer. The officials must also enforce rules regarding proper protective equipment, such as mouth guards, face protectors, and helmets. Players who fail to wear the required equipment should not be allowed in the game; if they are undetected at the beginning and discovered later, they should be removed from the game.

8. The athlete must be encouraged to report all injuries and not to hide them from his coach or his parents, for fear of ridicule or a seat on the bench for the next game. "It's a part of discipline," says Dr. Martin Blezina of Los Angeles. "It's a matter of convincing the child that reporting all injuries is the best thing for [him], and not the worst." At the same time, the parents have to be responsive to warning signals. They should be on the alert for the youngster who tries to cover up blisters and slight sprains; he may be hiding a more serious injury. The child who is always complaining about minor bumps and bruises may be telling his parents that he doesn't enjoy the sport as much as they think; he may be looking for a way to escape. In such an instance, forcing him to continue playing is not only an injustice to the child, but will alienate him from the sport even more, perhaps for the rest of his life.

Before their child ever gets involved in athletics, parents

should know the injury potential of the sport and should try to determine whether the child is physically and emotionally equipped for the stresses in store. If the child is basically timid, with an ungainly physique, forcing him into sports like football or hockey in order to "make him a man" is simply the wrong course. The child's fears and physique may lead to the very injuries he dreads. Similarly, if a boy is fast and loves soccer, what's to be gained—aside from father's ego investment—by pushing him into football, where the risk of injury, especially to the knee, is so much higher?

Following is a brief look at several of the sports where injuries are a concern.

Youth Football

Orthopedists and physicians are being joined by respected voices within the football establishment who question the values of tackle football, Pop Warner-style, for preadolescents. Ron Mix, a former All-Pro lineman at San Diego and now a pro football executive, has said: "I don't advocate junior high football. There is a maturation level that should be reached before contact, and as a general rule that doesn't come before the age of 15 or 16. I think bones and muscles, particularly neck muscles, should reach a stage of maturity where there will be no permanent damage in case of injury."

Joe Paterno, the Penn State coach, feels that midget football should be abolished:

Kids of junior high school age are just not ready, physically or emotionally, for an organized football program. . . . Very often they become victims of injuries. It doesn't matter how much protection they have in the way of equipment. Their bones are soft and they are still growing. They don't know how to protect themselves and they can get hurt so easily in a scrimmage or a game. Frequently they sustain injuries that bother them for the rest of their lives.

Pop Warner football is inherently safer than the game played in high school and beyond, just by the nature of play—boys playing against boys of similar weight and generating far less velocity at impact than their older counterparts. But the very real threat of injury still exists on every play. For one thing, man is simply not built for football. "If God had intended man to engage in strenuous sports, He would have given us better knees," said Dr. Robert Ray, head of orthopedic surgery at the University of Illinois College of Medicine in Chicago.

One safety measure in this area strongly advocated by Dr. Joseph Torg is the use of short, rounded soccer-style cleats in place of traditional football shoes. Torg's four-year experiment at the high school level in Philadelphia showed "a marked decrease in both the incidence and severity" of knee and ankle injuries when players switched from football shoes to soccer-style shoes. In one league the number of knees requiring surgery dropped dramatically from 32 to 4 in one season. As Torg says in *The Physician and Sportsmedicine*: "We recommend that the conventional shoe be condemned and replaced by a soccer-type shoe with the following specifications: (1) synthetic molded sole, (2) minimum of 14 cleats per shoe, (3) minimum cleat tip diameter of $\frac{1}{2}$ inch, and (4) maximum cleat length of $\frac{3}{8}$ inch." He explained that the shorter length and larger diameter of the soccer cleats, and their greater number (the normal football shoe has seven cleats) prevents deep penetration in the ground and thus greatly lessens the possibility of foot fixation, which is an important factor contributing to knee and ankle injuries.

Further steps should also be taken to cut the number of injuries resulting from inadequate protective equipment. Carl S. Blyth and Frederick O. Mueller, the University of North Carolina researchers who conducted a landmark four-year study of 8,776 high school football players in North Carolina, recommended in their report to the U.S. Consumer Product Safety Commission that: "Physicians, coaches and others responsible for athletic programs . . . must take a firm stand in demanding safer equipment. This would include requiring manufacturers to provide soft external padding of all helmets and shoulder pads to limit the injuries from blows delivered by the items." In addition, careful consideration should be given to proper mouthpieces, sturdy face guards, and well-fitting and adequate shoulder pads.

Every league should also impose guidelines to protect the injured youngster from overzealous, untrained coaches. Joel Adams helped formulate the following medical guidelines for the youth football program in his area:

1. A player sustaining any injury should leave the game and not play again until he has obtained medical clearance. Exceptions being superficial abrasions and scratches, or if he had "wind knocked out," providing this diagnosis is verified by a doctor on the field and internal injury ruled out.

2. Head injury with even a momentary loss of consciousness or headache automatically ruled out for the remainder of the season.

3. No player partially recovered from an injury may return to play taped, bandaged, or splinted in any way. There is absolutely no excuse to allow a player in this young age group to return to play until he is 100 percent recovered from his injury.

4. Grabbing face masks, spearing, and other deliberate infractions penalized 15 yards and ejection of the offending player from the game. According to Adams, "This was done primarily to prevent players from developing bad habits at this young age and to discourage overly aggressive coaching." Other medical experts argue that "spearing"—hitting the opponent with the head—should even be outlawed, since it leads to far too many head and neck injuries.

Ice Hockey

This is a sport where the coach tries to inculcate in each of his players the underlying values of aggression and violence. From the coach's perspective, the quicker a youngster can learn to willingly hurl his body around on the ice, the sooner he will become a good hockey player and the more valuable he will be to his team. Woe to the youngster—in the eyes of his coach, as well as his parents—who can't learn to deliver an effective body check or slam another player against the sideboards or fight for the puck in close quarters amid flailing sticks. The injuries that stem from these aggressive tactics are excused by hockey followers as "occupational hazards," and the youngsters who can't take it "don't belong in the sport." But there's no reason, aside from adult motivations, not to tone down the game at the preadolescent level so that youngsters could learn the fundamentals of the game such as stick handling, puck control, shooting, and passing without worrying about being decked by an opponent who thinks he's going to make it to the pros as an intimidator.

Fortunately, the most dangerous injuries in hockey—injuries to the head and face, such as lacerations, lost teeth, and skull fractures—can be largely prevented by proper head protection, firm officiating, and sensible coaching. For instance, players who are guilty of deliberate or unnecessary roughhousing or purposeful injury should simply be thrown out of the game, if not suspended for a number of games. There should be strict enforcement against body checking to the knees and head and from the blind side. And players should not be allowed on the ice without standard equipment such as shoulder and elbow guards and shin pads, as well as mouthpieces and helmets. Helmets should cover the ear and mastoid portion of the skull because of the poor protection of that area, according to Raymond W. Gibbs, assistant surgeon to the Harvard Athletic Association. He writes in *The Physician and Sportsmedicine*:

Almost all helmets leave the ears and the temporal area and its neighboring meningeal artery exposed. This is a serious defect in all designs. Almost all helmets give poorer protection to the frontal and occipital portions of the skull and have chin straps that are inadequate to keep the helmet in proper position when the player is struck.

An acceptable hockey helmet should have the following characteristics: (a) be lightweight, (b) have a stout suspension lining, (c) give adequate coverage to the frontal, temporal, and occipital portions of the skull, (d) have sturdy chin straps that fit firmly under the jaw to hold the helmet securely to the head, (e) be easily removable, (f) allow for proper circulation between the head and the helmet to prevent excessive heat buildup around the head. Helmets meeting these requirements should be made available without greatly increasing the cost of equipping the player.

Swimming

Young swimmers can suffer the same damage as Little League pitchers as a result of the constant pulling of the shoulder muscles on the growth line. Joel Adams even calls it "Swimmer's shoulders." Breaststrokers are especially susceptible to "breaststroker's knee," brought on by the tensions and stresses on the knee as it moves from flexion to extension. Two Canadian orthopedists, John C. Kennedy and Richard J. Hawkins, studied 2,496 competitive swimmers who swam an average of 5,000 yards per day, and of whom 261 had orthopedic complaints in the shoulder, knee, or calf and foot. All 70 knee problems were caused by the breaststroke. Their recommendation: that the breaststroke swimmer "should have at least two months of total rest per year when the knee joints are not subjected to these abnormal stresses."

Other injuries and ailments, such as tendonitis, ear and sinus infections, and loss of hair are resulting from the rigorous training regimen that has been self-inflicted as the price to pay to keep U.S. swimmers on top of the swimming world. Sacramento swim coach Sherm Chavoor, who once trained Mark Spitz and Debbie Meyer, acknowledged at the height of the 1974 season that even his star swimmers were complaining of ailments:

When your best people start backing off to pain you know it's real. This shoulder tendonitis is affecting more and more swimmers. This hair thing is for real, too. A lot of my kids are wearing bathing caps all the time—they've noticed their hair falling out. A dermatologist told me the chlorine content is stronger in many pools than it used to be.

Gymnastics

Although gymnastics is not a contact sport, the danger of injury is always present, especially while performing or practicing on the uneven parallel bars, the side horse, or the balance beam, where youngsters will bump into equipment or land awkwardly on the floor. There is also the risk of damage to the growth lines, especially in the spine and shoulders, resulting from the stresses and repetition of training in a competitive environment. Joel Adams warns that the gymnast (or any adolescent athlete for that matter) should never train according to the rule of thumb in swimming and long distance running, where the object is to practice until one's body is in pain—and then push through the pain. "This isn't true in gymnastics," he said. "If the child feels pain, the reason is more likely to be a growth line pain than a muscle pain, and the child has to back off."

Baseball

An official of the National Athletic Health Institute in Los Angeles estimates that up to 100,000 boys develop chronic elbow strain in a single year in Little League baseball. And Mike Marshall, one of baseball's top relief pitchers and a Ph.D. candidate in kinesiology, contends that youngsters who throw a baseball too hard too often too soon can become "virtual cripples" by their late teens. "What I think we have done over the past 20 years, by using adult rules in children's baseball programs, is we have selectively taken the best arms and ruined them," says Marshall. Yet, as Joel Adams points out, "Little Leaguer elbow has never been mentioned in published injury statistics by Little League headquarters. He further notes, "It is by far the most common and potentially serious condition associated with the sport, despite the fact that it is the easiest to prevent and treat, if recognized early."

"Little League elbow" is actually a group of five disorders affecting the growth elements in the pitching elbow, brought on by the abnormal repetitious movement of the arm during the pitching motion. A similar ailment can affect the pitching shoulder. In both cases pain persists when the youngster pitches. "Most cases respond to rest and abstinence from pitching," said Joseph Torg. The trouble comes when the coach or father tells the boy whose arm is sore to "pitch it out," or when the youngster fails to tell anyone that his arm is hurting. "In severe cases," said Torg, "healing may take up to a year or 18 months. Also, a fragment of bone may become detached, float free in the elbow joint, interfere with joint mechanics and cause life-long arthritic changes." Hall of Fame pitcher Sandy Koufax, who was forced into early retirement by an arthritic arm, once said: "A man's arm is not designed to go out and throw as hard as he can. I had pain in my arm most of my life. All pitchers do."

As a result of the study mentioned earlier, Joel Adams made the following recommendations for pitching at the Little League level:

1. Install pitching machines and let the pitcher field the position, or limit pitchers to 2 innings instead of 6.

2. Encourage pitchers to report shoulder or elbow pain immediately and to discontinue pitching [but may play other positions] until epiphyses are closed.

3. Advise pitchers not to practice throwing at home before, during, or off season as excessive throwing invites trouble, rather than perfection at this age.

4. Abolish curveball throwing as it not only puts an additional strain on the elbow but requires excessive throwing practice to perfect.

5. Educate parents and coaches that shoulder and elbow pain

at this age indicates epiphyseal [growth line] or joint involvement and should not be treated as routine muscle soreness found in adult pitchers following a game.

Adams was dismayed, for example, when one major league baseball trainer offered this advice to doctors who treat sore-elbowed Little Leaguers: "Tell him just not to throw hard for a while but to keep throwing. Then when the arm begins to feel better with less soreness, throw a little harder." Says Adams: "That's like telling someone with a sore toe to keep kicking the wall but just don't kick it as hard. A sore arm isn't muscle soreness in a youngster, it's a growth line problem and if you have him keep throwing you are only going to risk permanent injury."

Robert Kerlan and Marshall join Adams in criticizing the use of curve balls and sliders at the Little League level. "The unnatural contortions of the arm and elbow are harmful enough to the pros, to say nothing of young athletes whose bones and joints are still growing," said Kerlan. When Marshall lectures to sports medicine groups he uses a film shot of himself pitching. By stopping it at various positions during his windup, he shows how unnatural an act pitching is and the pressure it places on bone, cartilage, and muscle. "It's even worse in kids," he says. "We shouldn't put pressures on them that will ruin the development of their skeletal structures and lead to deformities." He adds that Little League pitchers tend to be the children with the best muscle development who can throw the hardest, and thus the players with the most athletic potential are the ones who are risking the greatest permanent damage.

The pressure on youngsters to throw as hard as possible poses yet another problem. "As a Little League parent and coach, you should teach control and a smooth, natural delivery," says Kerlan. "The most important pitch for a youngster is one that goes where he wants it to go, regardless of speed. Once a child gains control and can move the ball around the strike zone, he can start to deliver it a little faster.

But speed should never be attempted at the sacrifice of accuracy."

Adams also warns that medical studies of Little League elbow which end at age twelve can be highly misleading. "The problem comes on gradually," he says. "The major contributing cause is excessive repetitious trauma and these conditions seem to reach their peak at the Pony League age of thirteen or fourteen." Thus a youngster may pitch effectively in Little League, despite an occasional sore elbow, only to be suddenly sidelined for good when he reaches high school.

Unfortunately, as Dr. Allan J. Ryan wrote in *The Physician and Sportsmedicine*, in discussing the need for rigidly enforced rules that limit innings pitched—weekly and in a game—and condemning the use of curveballs: "Even these rules will fall short if enforced until basic attitudes change." He advocated the use of a pitching machine (discussed in chapter 15), which has led to improved batting averages, more runs, more defensive plays, in other words, more fun, while sore arms have been virtually eliminated in leagues where it has been employed. "As long as adults control and dominate these organized baseball programs for adolescents," Ryan continued, "it seems unlikely that any of the other proposed control measures short of this will solve the problem. Limitation of innings pitched or batters faced is nullified by extra hours of throwing practice at home encouraged by fathers and older brothers." Even the matter of warming up before the game can add two or three innings of strain if the youngster tries to emulate a big league pitcher by throwing hard for ten or fifteen minutes. "Kids are active all day," Adams points out. "They don't need to loosen up their muscles like an adult."

Joseph Torg is equally dismayed by the competitive Little League environment which, he feels, encourages "the tendency to treat physically and emotionally immature youngsters as adults." In 1973 he compared the findings by Adams with those from a study he helped conduct on the effects of pitching on the arms of participants in an inner-city youth baseball program in Philadelphia. The Lighthouse Boys' Club program (ages nine to eighteen) is organized "to encourage participation and recreation rather than to ferment intense competition," Torg wrote. Teams are arbitrarily chosen at the beginning of each season, and each player must play at least three and a half innings of every game. Each pitcher is allowed to pitch seven innings each week, and curveball pitching is allowed. Nevertheless, after a full season of play, roentgenographic examinations of the shoulders and elbows of 44 of the 49 pitchers showed no shoulder abnormalities and only two instances of elbow damage.

In trying to compare pitching in Little League and pitching in the Lighthouse program, Torg believed that the major difference is the circumstances under which the two groups participate. "Specifically, Little Leaguers must compete to make the team, must compete to play in each game, and are subjected to intense pressures to win by adult coaches and spectators. On the other hand, all the Lighthouse Boys' Club members are automatically assigned to a team and must play at least three and one-half innings of each game. The general attitude is one of participation for the sake of recreation rather than competition."

In view of the evidence presented in this chapter, what can the coach do if he has a twelve-year-old pitcher who is tall and strong, with an overpowering fastball and the desire to pitch every inning possible? The coach realizes that if the boy ever hopes to pitch in college, let alone the major leagues, he may be pitching on borrowed time. But the boy is thinking only of the present; he likes the glory and being the center of attention, and his parents are basking in his success; he makes them important figures in their local Little League. So what does the coach do who is more interested in this boy's future as an athlete than he is in a Little League championship?

First of all, the coach should talk to the boy and explain what he wants to do, and why. "From what I've read, and what I've heard from doctors, if you continue to pitch every game, you're going to ruin your arm. So I'd like you to learn to play a couple of other positions and concentrate more on your hitting. This will make you a better all-around player. This doesn't mean that you'll never pitch this year. I'll let you pitch a couple of innings in our important games. But I want to help see that you still have a healthy arm in high school."

The coach would then talk to the parents in a similar manner. "Your son has been an excellent pitcher the last two years, but I'm concerned that he may throw his arm out. I can understand if you're disappointed, but I think it's important to take a few precautions now. Besides, what does he have to prove? We know he's the best pitcher in the league."

If the coach is opposed by the parents, he should tell them, "If you want your boy to pitch every game, then you should have him play with another team. I won't take that responsibility with his arm." But I think most families are sensible enough to realize that if a coach is this serious about their son's future, and is obviously well informed, they must go along with his decision.

12

The Coach

THE BEST-INTENTIONED efforts by parents and many of the potential benefits of sports at the preadolescent level can either be bolstered or come unraveled at the hands of the coach and his assistants. Some parents will argue that the coach doesn't really wield that much influence—"Kids don't listen to adults, they go their own way"—but this is to ignore the powerful impact the coach can have during the season. For one thing, the coach in a team sport represents the authority figure making important decisions involving the child. The youngster wants to play, but the coach decides whether or not he starts, and controls how long he will stay in the game or sit on the bench. Secondly, if the child's ideal is athletics, the coach is as important as the teacher in many cases. He can motivate the child to learn the skills of the sport and strive for improvement. Or he can crush the child's spirit with constant criticisms and deprecations. Third, the coach is a model to the child simply by what he says, his mannerisms, his response to the joys and stresses of competition. This will shape the child's own sense of reward or futility from participating in sports.

The good coach on the preadolescent level will have many of the attributes of a good father. He's always there. He's sensitive to emotions. The child's performance is important and he'll push the child to improve, but he cares about the child as a human being first and an athlete second. He wants the child to learn the fundamentals and enjoy the sport, regardless of team victories or personal triumphs along the way. Instead of emulating hard-nosed "big league" coaches, he tries to be a nice, lovable, concerned guy while also being firm and well organized, because that's what youngsters respond to at that age. They're thinking, "If he knows who I am, if I know I'm going to play regularly, if I know he's concerned about me and it's fun, I don't really care that much about the final score."

In the sensibly run leagues, with sensible parents, a coach with these qualities will be encouraged and supported even if he never has a winning season. The parents recognize that his contribution to their child's growth is invaluable. He is, in fact, like a third parent, a strong adult model who can have a marked bearing on the child's life.

Alas, too few coaches at the preadolescent level have a philosophy of coaching that keeps the child's emotional needs foremost in mind. Imbued with the professional-collegiate model, they harass the umpires and officials, shout at their players, give them inane pep talks, belittle their mistakes, administer punishment drills, and in general display the symptoms of someone who's only goal is to win. They operate on the notion that no one player is more important than the team, and thus place league championships, even a winning season, ahead of the psyches of eleven-year-old athletes.

In all fairness to these coaches, most of them are caught in a difficult predicament. Many are volunteers just trying to do their civic duty. They may be coaching because their child is playing or because they once participated in a certain sport. They may have fantasized themselves as football or baseball strategists for many years, and now here's their chance to put their living room theories into practice and to get instant feedback from a group of preadolescents. Whatever the reasons, most of them have minimal experience as a coach (let alone training in child psychology) and they have very poor models to copy—college and pro coaches who are in the public eye, on television or in the news media. They ape the behavior of these coaches and adopt their trite clichés, such as "Winners never quit and quitters never win" and "When the going gets tough, the tough get going." Meanwhile, the coaching qualities that are most effective and most important at the childhood level—concern, understanding, patience, an even temper—are often completely overlooked or downplayed as the coach formulates his philosophy—if, indeed, he even makes the effort to sit down and think through his attitudes and his goals.

One purpose of the following three chapters, therefore, is to suggest attitudes and approaches to make the coach more sensitive, and thus more effective in coping with the emotions of his young ball players. Just as it is important for coaches to teach the correct techniques and impart a respect for the fundamentals of the sport, it is equally vital that they develop a more humanistic approach to coaching. My goal here is not to help coaches improve their won-lost record or to produce more individual champions, but to help them develop better young people through sports participation. If coaches only search these chapters for "tricks" to help them win more games, then I've simply contributed to the madness I deplore.

Parental Assessment of the Coach

Despite the coach's obvious influence, many parents fail to make an effort to find out what kind of person is dealing with their youngster's psyche. They will help their child register for a sport, drop him off for practice, and then show up for all the games, confident that they are on top of his activity. But all they know about the coach is that he makes a lot of noise during the game, he argues with the officials, and he writes things down on a clipboard, so he obviously wants to win. However, if parents are serious about wanting their child to get as much out of sports as possible, then they must take steps to determine the coach's attitudes towards children, the approach he uses in working with them, and his own philosophy about competition and the relative importance of winning, at this level of participation. The latter will give a strong indication as to whether or not the child will have a positive experience in athletics, even though he might be a substitute or his team a loser. The parents should also realize that it is entirely possible for their child to be on a winning team and still feel the experience was extremely negative because of a harsh, unrelenting approach by the coach.

MEETINGS AT THE LEAGUE LEVEL

Parents should arrange a meeting with all the coaches and officials so that everybody involved can discuss the goals and philosophy of the league. For instance, parents will want to know if league officials and the majority of coaches take a hard-line attitude towards competition. Are there measures to ensure that everybody gets to play in every game? Will trophies be given to the leading players? Will everybody on the championship team get a trophy?

Obviously there will be philosophical conflicts, between parents and coaches and among the parents themselves. Some parents will state, "Look, we want our kids to win. We want them to be on top. That should be the goal for every coach." But others will counter, "Hey, wait a minute. Maybe we ought to just think about the kids participating and having fun." Those who want to de-emphasize winning could remind the competitive hard hats: "Here's what we're doing. We're playing all season so that only one team will get a trophy. They'll be called the winners and everyone else will be called losers. Is this what we really want?" (In some leagues, post-season awards are not a trivial matter. When Cleveland

Little League manager Mike Constantino refused to name a most valuable player on his team, he was dismissed by the Euclid Boys League because one of their rules mandates selection of an MVP by every manager. Constantino argued that he had an obligation to all fifteen boys on the team. "I can't allow one boy to inflate his ego and undermine what we have built up," he said. A league official replied, "Mike is a fine man and a fine manager. It's just that we have rules.")

Many leagues, unfortunately, are dominated by parents who have talented youngsters. These parents are deeply involved as coaches and league officers and they comprise a vocal minority which endorses the supposed character-building qualities of tough competition and the all-out quest for winning. Translated, this means the best players should play as long as possible in every game. The parents of a budding superstar seldom care about the less talented players; they simply want their youngster to look good, to play on the all-star team and then move up to the next level. Ideally, however, a meeting with all the parents will help minimize these conflicts, since the boy on the bench will be represented as well as the superstar.

The coach will have to contend with the pressures from both sides. He may, in fact, be in sympathy with one faction or the other. But it will be easier for him, and the parents, if everyone knows where they stand before the season begins, instead of waiting for conflicts to erupt once play is under way.

DISCUSSIONS AT THE TEAM LEVEL

A meeting or a backyard picnic should also be arranged so that all the players and parents can gather informally to talk to the coach about the team and the season ahead. The parents should find out personally what kind of coach they have by asking him such questions as: What is his philosophy about winning and competition? Why is he coaching? What is his attitude towards substitutes and those with little talent? What are his goals for the season and how does he plan to carry them out? If the coach says, "Look, I'm out here to win, and this is the way I'm going to do it" or "My goal is to produce Olympic champions," then at least they have an honest coach; he's not trying to buffalo them with clichés. But the parents should try pinning him down. If he wants a team that goes all out for the league championship, what happens to the youngsters who ride the bench? Will they be given a chance to show what they can do other than make token appearances? It's fine for the coach to profess his need to win, but only if he supports *all* of his players, gives everybody a fair chance to play, and can respond maturely to defeat. The Pop Warner-Little League coach who gets his team to the top has usually done so at the expense of some nice children. That is why leagues have had to impose rules that everybody must play in every game—to help protect the eager but untalented youngster from the coach who is absolutely dedicated to winning.

COACH–PARENT COMMUNICATION

If nobody organizes a meeting at the league or team level, then the individual parents must arrange to talk with the coach on their own. Not to tell him what to do—he has enough headaches already and deserves a free hand in running his team—but to discuss the areas suggested above. The parents should use this opportunity to tell the coach what they hope their child can get out of the sport. It may be they want to keep him out of trouble, they want him to get exercise, or they want him to learn about the value of teamwork and setting goals. Perhaps the child has trouble controlling his emotions and the parents hope the coach and the sport will provide an environment that will bring him to greater maturity.

Oftentimes parents are afraid to interfere with the coach on a one-to-one basis. Either they don't want to force themselves on the coach or he makes it clear he doesn't feel any obligation to communicate, unless a parent can catch him walking off the field after a game or after practice. As we will see, wariness towards parental interference can be a well-founded fear in many coaches. Either the parents feel their youngster is not being given sufficient playing time, or they worry that junior isn't getting enough individual attention by the coach and his assistants in regard to technique. Instead of developing a friendly basis of communication with the coach, these parents often resort to writing letters or making nasty phone calls. Or they will confront the coach directly on the field: "Why isn't my Johnny starting? He's better than anybody you've got at that position." The coach has to be personally secure and have confidence in his coaching approach in order to withstand these pressures, let alone the scrutiny and questioning by parents. He must also realize the importance of his own efforts to initiate and encourage dialogue with the parents by making himself available. Such communication between the coach and the parents is vital to the success of any sports program for children. It takes up everybody's time, but I think it's obligatory for the parents and coaches to make this time, not only at the beginning of the year but as the season progresses.

Personal Observation by the Parents

It's one thing to listen to the coach expound his philosophy around the barbecue pit. But what happens to his thoughtful ideas once play begins and the pressure is on? Do they get shuffled aside in the expediency of winning? Is the coach, in fact, an entirely different person on the sidelines or in the dugout? To find out, the parents need to observe the coach during a game and at practice and to get feedback from their child.

For instance, the coach's language may change. He may think he has to shout and swear at his players to provide motivation and maintain discipline. He may seem like a nice guy, but when somebody goofs off or the game is being lost, his true colors show: he ridicules, scolds, and threatens his players and rages at the umpire. The most dangerous coaches, in fact, are those who appear to be relaxed and loosey-goosey until suddenly, in an important game, they go berserk. Totally confused by this inconsistency, their poor players are always on edge and afraid to strike out or make a blunder, never knowing when the coach is going to try to humiliate them into a better performance.

A friend of mine coaches Little League with a good-guy, low-keyed approach straight down the line. "I'm a zealot about this," he said. "I can't stand it when I see coaches yelling at their kids, especially in front of everybody. Sometimes after a game I'll even go up to a kid who has been chewed out by his coach and try to give him a little encouragement." I asked my friend how many other coaches in the league took his approach. "We have eight coaches and two others are like me. I thought there was a third, until I saw him banging his head against home plate protesting a call."

The parents therefore should observe if the coach is sensitive to the child's emotions following a crucial error, a fumble, several missed lay-ups, or repeated bad plays. Another good clue is to watch how the coach responds during a slump, or when his team loses all season long. Some coaches are apt to get depressed and take their frustrations out on the players. Others try to make it fun no matter what the score or how badly they're losing. Some coaches reject their players after a loss, others are quite supportive.

The parents will also want to know how the coach treats his players at practice. Is he abusive and hard driving, working his players until their tongues are dragging? "I'm not pushing these boys, they want all of this. They know this is what it takes to win." Or does he always vary the routine, keeping drills short, snappy, and well organized, with everybody active and very little standing around? The good coach will have the knack of working his players hard at meaningful fundamentals, but still have them enjoy it. He'll have a sense of humor, not a sense of frustration.

One obvious danger in encouraging parents to hang around

practice is that they pose a constant, second-guessing menace to the coach. Some fathers will even walk up to the coach in front of the players and ask why their son is not starting, or seeing more action, because he's obviously better than the kid playing ahead of him. The boy may agree with his father but he is incredibly embarrassed to have him interfere. Most young athletes want the *support* of their parents but they also want to know, "If I'm going to make it, I want to make it on my own." Another problem arises when parents show up at every practice and become friendly with the coaches. Pretty soon there's an unspoken pressure on the coach to see that so-and-so's youngster plays more. This not only gives the youngster a false sense of importance, but is quickly picked up by the other players and can undermine the regard they have for their coach.

The underlying key is for the parents to feel free to show their interest by coming out to practice, but only to observe, not to interfere. If the coach needs an assistant, he'll ask for volunteers.

By talking with their youngster, the parents can also learn if the coach's behavior is different at practice when there are a lot of parents around. Is he a little more careful about what he says? Is he a little less hostile and a lot more friendly in his general attitude? On the other hand, some coaches will try to play a tough-guy, I'm-in-charge role when being observed by a number of parents, thinking this is what they want to see, especially in football.

Ultimately, through conversations with the coach, their own personal observations, and contributions from their child, parents can learn if the coach's overriding concern is simply the end result—who wins and who loses—or the benefits along the way: trying to help each athlete learn the game and improve while having fun, despite the team's relative success or failure. The parents will also be able to know if the coach places the welfare of the child first and his own personal needs (winning, titles, champions) second.

If this order is reversed and the coach is having a strong negative influence on their child, what can parents do? (1) They continue to support the child and let him know they understand what he is going through. (2) They should talk to the coach and explain why they are dissatisfied. There's a fine line at work here between the coach's right to decide who plays and for how long, and the parents' right to question the way he deals with the emotions of their child. (3) If other players on the team are unhappy and are being insensitively handled by the coach, then all the parents affected should arrange a meeting with the coach in order to bring their complaints into the open. Perhaps the coach is unaware that his coaching style alienates so many of his players; his team may be leading the league and he simply assumes that even the bench warmers are happy to be on a winner. Alerted to morale problems, he may promise to make changes. More than likely, however, he will argue that this is the way he has always coached and if the parents don't like it, they can pull their boy off the team—which means the boy is the one who suffers, no matter what happens. (4) If the coach claims he doesn't have enough time to manage the team while also working out personality problems, the parents should volunteer their services at practice to help free the coach to spend more time talking with individual players and building a rapport. (5) If the coach refuses to change his approach, the parents should protest to the league president. Once again, though, I want to emphasize that the coach's won-lost record must never be the issue, nor the strategy he might employ during games. The crucial measurement must be the child's physical and emotional well-being. (6) Failing all else, the parents should allow their child to leave the team at any point. The child could try another sport or hope for a better coach the following season.

The Father as Coach

One of the problems facing kids' leagues everywhere is the shortage of competent coaching volunteers, especially those who know something about child raising as well as the techniques of the sport. Thus leagues very often must turn to the fathers who have youngsters playing on a team.

Although I have seen many fathers develop into excellent coaches under these circumstances, I would recommend that a father coach another team, unless he feels he can handle the pressures that are bound to arise. For when a father chooses to coach his own youngster, he puts himself in a terrible bind.

If the father lacks confidence in his coaching ability, and tries not to alienate anybody, he will often play his son less than his ability warrants. In which case the message to his son is clear: "These people are more important to me than you are." But if the father's main concern is that his son play all the time, often in the glamour positions and regardless of his ability, then the son may feel protected, but certain parents are bound to grumble—"Harvey's always playing his own kid"— and the players who ride the bench can be counted on to use Harvey's kid as a fall guy.

The father who insists on coaching his own child must learn to evaluate his child's skills the best he can, and give him the same amount of playing time as the other players at his ability level. The father needs to let his son know that everybody on the team has to be treated fairly, but that whatever decisions are made are not a personal thing.

What the father really needs is an objective assessment from someone he can trust, hopefully the assistant coach. He needs to ask this person, "Look, how do you really view my kid? Very honestly, do you think he should be playing more, or less? Should he even be starting?" A similar dilemma exists for the assistant coach who has a child on the team. He wants his boy to play but he doesn't want to push, and thus he is always walking a very fine line.

Further Pressures on the Coach

Many critics of childhood sports like to make fall guys out of coaches. They argue that most coaches either don't know what they are doing or undermine the benefits that sports can provide by applying devastating pressures on young psyches and growing bodies. I'll agree that there are too many coaches who are working out their problems and their fantasies through the youngsters they coach, sincere as they might be in their belief that tough competition and insistent, unyielding coaching will help their athletes prepare for life. However, we can't overlook one constant reality of childhood sports—the insanity of pushing parents and the ways they can undermine even the strongest, most personally secure coaches.

Whenever I give a speech to coaches or managers, one of them invariably comes up afterwards and tells me, in kind of an apologetic, hiding way, "Look, I believe very much in what you're saying. But where I come from they're giving me a rough time because I'm not emphasizing winning."

I once dealt with a high school football coach in the San Jose area whose dilemma typified such pressures. He was the kind of coach most of us would have liked to play under. He was concerned about all his players, he wouldn't shame them into playing with injuries, he spent time talking with them and meeting with their families, and he had a low-keyed coaching style by means of which he rejected the win-or-else, losing-is-hell philosophy of most of his coaching rivals. His players grew as persons in this environment, they liked their coach, and they liked the sport, even though they weren't big "winners" on the scoreboard, generally losing as many games as they won. This was the coach's downfall. He unfortunately happened to be working in a community that was permeated with football mania. The school was relatively new and the townsfolk were hoping to build an "athletic tradition," i.e., they wanted to win. Finally a group of "concerned" parents went to the principal to "encourage" him to change football coaches.

Now the principal was on the spot. He liked the coach and agreed with his approach, although he admitted he wished it could have produced a league champion or two. Under repeated pressures, however, the principal finally had to call the coach in and tell him, "You're going to have to produce a winner or you'll have to leave."

"That's not my style," the coach protested. "I can't start pushing these kids beyond their capacity."

Those critics who have a natural inclination to come down hard on coaches should ask themselves, What was this coach going to do? Where could he turn for support? Who could really understand his position? If he stayed humanistic but failed to produce a winner, he would lose his job. If he turned insane and started driving his players to exhaustion, he might win more ball games, but he would hate himself and he would lose the humanistic rapport he had built up with his players.

The coach refused to buckle his convictions. When the season ended, he resigned and went back into teaching.

Parents can undermine the coach in other, more subtle ways, often without realizing the damage they are doing and the conflicts they are causing. In most cases the young athlete gets caught in the middle and is the one who suffers. Some examples:

1. The boy is the high school quarterback and his father is a well-known former coach. At the beginning of fall practice the father asks his son about the team's offense and the boy explains, somewhat sheepishly, that the coach wants to emphasize the running game. He sketches a few plays. "Look, you can't do that," says the father. "You've got a hell of a passing arm. They've got to use that arm." So the youngster goes out to the practice field with his father's admonition in the back of his head. But the coach keeps working on the running game, with only an occasional pass. Once the season starts, the halfbacks are making all the headlines while the quarterback just hands off, and every game the father continues to chew his son out for not throwing more passes.

The youngster is caught in what I call the Athletic Triangle—a conflict which involves the coach, the athlete, and his father or mother. In this instance the boy can't tell his father, "Look, I have to listen to the coach. He's the one who calls the plays." The father would probably accuse him of lacking courage to speak up to the coach about his ability to thrŏw the ball. Yet the boy can't tell the coach, "Could you get my father off my back? He thinks we should be passing a lot more. He's really giving me a rough time." This could be seen as a sign of weakness on the boy's part, that he wasn't able to handle the pressure. And besides, the coach is already sensitive to interference by the father. So the boy is stuck in the middle, and both sides are driving him crazy. The only healthy way out is for open lines of communication to exist among the coach, the parents, and the athlete. Otherwise the coach may not even be aware of the boy's dilemma. Wherever conflicts exist between parent and coach in the area of strategy, the coach must obviously have the final word, even if the father is convinced he knows what's best. In the case cited above, the father was also worried about his son's chances of winning a college football scholarship.

The sensible father will handle a situation of this kind the way former pro quarterback Rudy Bukich did with his son Steve, who was the senior starting quarterback for Newport Harbor High, California, in 1973. Young Bukich stood six feet one and weighed 200 pounds, and his coach even admitted, "He's the best high school passer I have ever seen in this area." The coach, however, lived by the run, and Bukich passed only about twelve times a game for a winning team. But this lack of passing opportunities didn't bother Bukich's father, who said:

I don't want to butt in. The coaches know what they are doing. It's none of my business, in a sense. I'm interested in my boy. But I'm also interested in the success of the team. Sure I'd like to see Steve throw more. But at the right time, the right field position, the right pattern. I don't want to see him throw just for the sake of throwing.

2. The boy plays basketball and his father is a former player. The boy is a guard and his father begins to tell him how to play the position—which is contrary to what the coach is

teaching. Pretty soon the boy is all fouled up. He can't tell his father and he can't tell his coach. He winds up playing so poorly that the coach has to bench him. Sometimes, in fact, the athlete who is squeezed between his coach and his parents will simply give up and let himself be benched or thrown off the team so that both sides will at least get off his back temporarily.

3. The coach and the player are both so embarrassed by the father's actions that they don't know how to handle him. The father comes to a game and his mouth is like a megaphone. At the top of his voice he's yelling down instructions, chewing out the coach and criticizing his son. The father is so overbearing that he actually drives the athlete and the coach closer together. One day the coach even admits to the boy, with a grin, "Your father is really on both of us, isn't he? I mean, he's really giving us a rough time." The boy is embarrassed but relieved to know that the coach understands and is on his side.

Another variation of the Athletic Triangle comes when the parents are a little worried about their own needs and their own abilities as parents. Let's say I love my son very much and I send him off to play with Red Magoo. Pretty soon my son starts coming home at night and saying, "Boy, Coach Magoo is the most wonderful person in the world. He's the greatest guy I've ever met." All of a sudden, as a parent, I'm a little less. If only I could be Red Magoo. This is not an unrealistic problem, either, because Red Magoo is obviously meeting my boy's emotional needs and giving him something I can't give him or haven't given him. This realization is a threat to some parents. In fact, it takes a very mature parent to say, "He really must be a wonderful guy. I'll have to see what he does and try to learn something."

Instead, how do many parents respond who feel threatened? They try to find faults. If the team starts losing, they are quick to point out, "Magoo's not so hot after all." If the team keeps winning but the son is not playing every inning, they wonder out loud, "Why isn't the coach playing you? You're the best outfielder on the team." Some parents will even go so far as to pull their youngster off the team, they are so threatened by what is happening.

In some instances and in certain locales, the coach may find himself confronted by the stereotype of the coach who is supposed to be hard-driving and bent on ultimate victory. If the coach has a low-keyed, sympathetic approach, he may be second-guessed not only by parents but also by his own players, who wonder why they aren't being pushed. Obviously, the younger the child the less this will be anticipated, but as they get older they might simply expect an aggressive coach. Their parents are pushing them and they see the other coaches pushing their players. If they are losing more games than they win, they might figure the coach is at fault. Such was the case of a Little Leaguer who wrote a letter to the Atlanta Braves front office:

Dear Braves,

Our coach says that the most important thing is not just to win but to play fair. So far we haven't won any games. How can we get a coach that plays a little dirty?

13

Common Coaching Dilemmas

IDEALLY, all coaches should be required to take courses in interpersonal relations, child development, and human values. They need to be aware of the psychological pitfalls in high-pressure, organized sports for children and to realize that in the course of a season they may face more immediate child-rearing problems than the parents. In reality, however, most coaches at the preadolescent level rarely have any formal training in child psychology. They deal with emotional problems by drawing on their own athletic experiences, on the way they were coached, on the way they are raising their children, on what they observe of other coaches, and on what they read in the sports pages or coaching books. Obviously, this hit-and-miss, seat-of-the-pants approach makes it difficult for them to do everything right or to know all the answers. The purpose of this chapter is not to supply them with answers, since the list of problems can be endless, but to discuss many of the common personality and competitive situations that might challenge them during the season and to provide some possible approaches that will lead to more productive behavior.

The Shy, Introverted Athlete

Every coach eventually has to deal with the timid youngster who has a crushed or passive ego, the boy, for instance, who has been dominated by older brothers and sisters, or intimidated by his father, or bossed by his mother while the father didn't care or was too busy making a living. The boy is probably out for a sport because somebody in the family thought it would be a good way for him to learn to become more aggressive. A youngster like this can be easily ignored or passed over unless the coach is sensitive to what is happening. The child will hide in the background and rarely let himself be known. He may want to play but he doesn't have the courage to be able to speak out. He will wait to be picked rather than volunteer and will play wherever the coach puts him, which will usually be the sport's equivalent of right field.

A child like this needs emotional support from a sympathetic coach. He needs to know that the coach is going to back him. The last thing he needs is a browbeating. But if he has a tough-minded coach, that is what could happen. When this coach was an athlete himself and was criticized by a coach, his response was, "Boy, I'm going to show him!" But for him now to start shouting at an overly sensitive youngster whenever the boy makes mistakes—thinking this will motivate him—is senseless and counterproductive; the boy will simply feel rejected and withdraw even more. *The coach needs to know this.* Tough-minded coaches find it difficult enough to empathize with athletes of this nature, and they make it obvious they would much rather have a team of hard-nosed competitors—a mirror image of themselves.

A similar awareness is needed by the coach if the introverted youngster is playing a sport that has physical contact, such as football, or one that has a fearful element, such as facing a fastball pitcher in baseball. The child who is frightened of the aggressive aspects of sports needs support and encouragement; he does not need to have the coach wound his already fragile pride by calling him a sissy or a coward. In Little League, for instance, youngsters who are afraid of a fast ball pitcher give themselves away. They line up properly, in the middle of the batter's box, but as they wait for the pitch they're shuffling their feet backwards. By the time the pitch comes in, they're out of the box, safely away from the plate. They can't even reach the plate with their bat, but they really have no intention of swinging. Their message very clearly is "I don't want to be hit."

The responsibility of the coach in this case is to tell the youngster before his next turn at bat: "Look, I know he's a fast pitcher. But I want you to go up there and dig in. I don't care if you hit the ball or not, but you have to learn to stand in at the plate, okay? Next thing, I don't want you to swing at the first two pitches. Just get used to seeing the ball come in. After two pitches, make sure you see the ball coming right down the middle. Don't swing at anything else. If you swing at anything else, I think you're going to miss it. If it's down the middle and you miss, it's my fault. Don't worry." By doing this the coach is not only helping the child face an intimidating situation, but he is assuming any burden of error and thus helping the child concentrate.

Just talking to the youngster like this will relieve much of his tension. All the pressure is taken off his shoulders to hit the ball. He knows that all he has to do is look at the first two pitches and then look for a pitch right down the middle. If he knows that his coach will be proud of him just for staying in the box, he'll gradually acquire the needed confidence. But to think that a hitter is developed by making fun of him when he swings at a pitch over his head, or ridiculing him when he jumps out of the box, is sheer fantasy on the coach's part.

The Child Who Lacks Emotional Control

There are numerous manifestations of the lack of emotional control: the child gets hotheaded when he doesn't get his way; he pouts; he cries easily when he is frustrated or fails to perform properly; he has an inability to concentrate; or lets his feelings interfere with getting a job done.

Sports should be an area where the parents and coach can work together to correct behavior patterns such as these in the young athlete. Before the season starts the parents should warn the coach, "I'm afraid Freddie has temper tantrums when he doesn't get his way." The coach can then try to preempt Freddie's outbursts by telling his players at the first team meeting: "This is a team and we're all going to learn to play together. When we practice you have to learn to share and to take turns without fighting or arguing. We're going to have to work together in handling our feelings." Meanwhile, as the year progresses, the coach should recognize those occasions when Freddie displays controlled behavior; he should pull him aside after practice and say, "Freddie, I know it was tough for you today. We had a lot of drills you didn't like, and some of the guys were really on your back, but you stayed cool and you did a good job, and I'm really proud of you." At the same time Freddie's parents are tackling the problem at home, using similar methods of recognition and reward when Freddie displays the proper behavior.

Contrast this positive approach, however, to the reaction by many parents when behavior problems become apparent. Some parents want the coach to take charge of the youngster and make everything right, without a corresponding effort on their part. They view the coach as a child "trainer," especially regarding behavior they feel helpless to deal with. The coach is given the job of "straightening him out." They will say, "You go ahead and punish him, coach. You'll get our support. Go ahead and zonk him 'cause the kid's got to learn discipline."

Other parents have the tendency to cover up any problems

that might be embarrassing to them. They fail to warn the coach ahead of time and when the bad behavior starts occurring, the coach suddenly jumps all over the youngster, increasing the problem in an area where he needs help. Some coaches are even afraid they have brought on the problem and avoid telling the parents. A painful situation thus arises where both parties want change in the youngster, yet they hide the obvious facts from each other because they are unable to communicate.

In trying to overcome these problems in an enlightened environment, the coach should spend an equal amount of time periodically talking with each athlete, alone, as the season progresses. He should discuss what he is working toward in the youngster ability-wise as well as emotionally. He can also use an assistant or a volunteer to give special time to the child during practice. Another method to bring about healthy behavior on the team is to openly recognize the athlete who shows stability or a trait the coach wants the rest of the players to pick up. Use this athlete as a model: "That was a terrific job, Fenwick. I like the way you hung in there. That was great the way you handled that situation." Children are often very susceptible to models—peers as well as adults—and they will soon begin to emulate behavior the coach has praised. They now know what the guidelines are and what the coach wants.

Furthermore, the coach and the parents are important models. They must handle difficult situations in a mature way if they expect similar maturity in their children. Such an approach is rare in the world of sports today, but it could be practiced by every team, every athlete, every coach, and every parent in the country.

The Bully

The bully is not just a youngster who beats up on others in order to get his way. His actions are much broader than that. He can be a bully simply by constantly one-upping people. He doesn't hurt anybody physically, but he still ends up getting what he's after. He is obstreperous and at times obnoxious; he is constantly interfering, always volunteering, always pushing himself to the front of the line. When he's faced with a frustrating situation, aggression is his way out, physically or verbally.

Following are ways the coach can try to cope with the bully in the hopes of producing greater maturity in him.

The coach should keep in mind that if he demonstrates the same aggressive traits he is trying to curb, he simply sanctions the boy's behavior.

He should have a discussion with the boy and point out that he will be working on the problem during the season. He should explain why he feels the boy is a bully and point out that terrorizing other boys is not productive behavior.

As each incident comes up, the coach talks it out with the boy. They discuss what is happening and the child has a chance to explain and to defend himself. The coach has to be consistent. He can't talk to the child one day and ignore the same behavior the next.

It is vital that the boy knows the coach is aware of any improvement being made. The coach should recognize incidents where control is shown and let the boy know that he's proud of the way he handled his emotions under stress.

An open discussion should be held with the parents. The coach may discover that the parents actually take great pride in their child's aggressiveness; they don't even see the child as being a bully. On the other hand, the coach may be the one who is promoting aggression. He may feel that even if it is wildly unchanneled, it can make an important contribution to the team's competitive frame of mind.

The Hyperactive Child

The hyperactive child is unable to settle down for any period of time. He tends to be continually fidgeting and moving around. If he gets into any kind of activity, his mind is like a butterfly, quickly flitting off to something else. He cannot keep several different bits of information in his head simultaneously. If he is given two or three things to do immediately, he falls apart and loses interest.

The coach who can deal effectively with a youngster of this sort should be given medals for valor and high achievement. Actually, he is literally forced to cope with the situation. If he fails to channel the free-floating energies and anxieties of the hyperactive child, he may become a nervous wreck, and his practices could become a shambles. The child will find it almost impossible to concentrate on his particular job and will always want to be doing something else or playing another position.

One recommendation is to keep the child constantly occupied, but with a minimal amount of thinking required. Any type of physical activity, whether it be practicing sliding into a base or chasing fly balls, becomes a productive way of handling the overactive child. Do not make the assignment complex. Too many bits of information can only lead to chaotic reactions. Secondly, because his attention span is too easily distracted if he is always with the group, the child should be given a chance to work by himself on a specific skill. This is where the volunteer assistant can be invaluable. He (or she) should spend time with the child and give him the personal contact and attention that is crucial to bringing about greater individual control. The assistant will need unusual patience and a strong degree of calm in order to help the child learn to face the give-and-take with other children. If the child fails to respond with cooperative behavior, everybody will suffer.

Sports can be a valuable asset for the hyperactive child, but only in the situation where he has a narrow focus of responsibility and is kept physically active in a sport requiring gross muscle movement, such as soccer, basketball, hockey, or skiing. To place the child in a sport that calls for concentration over a period of time, in which he has to repeat fine muscle movement as well as complicated techniques—such as golf, gymnastics, or diving—is inappropriate and will produce more problems than benefits.

The Child Who Is Pressured by His Parents

Throughout this book I have discussed various examples of parental pressures on the child and the many difficulties that can result from such pressures. The coach must deal not only with the effect these pressures have on each athlete, but also with the initial suspicion of most young athletes that he (the coach) is simply an agent of the parents. A crucial goal of the coach, therefore, must be to convince each athlete that he is on his side, helping him to make the team and learn the sport, as opposed to keeping him from playing or inflicting the same punishing regimen that exists at home. The coach must prove to the child that he is genuinely concerned about helping him enjoy the sport and that he's not going to add to the pressures being applied by the parents. He makes it clear that the child will be evaluated on what he does at practice or in a game, and that he's not going to make him run ten laps because he failed math or keeps a sloppy bedroom. All the coach asks for is that the athlete work to his potential and have fun. Learning the skills of the sport and executing these skills under stress is tough enough on any youngster.

The coach should strive, in essence, to become the "good parent" or the "happy parent," rather than the "pressure parent." For example, through discussions with the parents and by observing their reactions during the game, a coach can generally sense how much pressure is being put on the child. If he knows that Fenwick's parents are on his back, when he makes a crucial mistake that costs the team a victory, the coach will be sensitive enough to step in and put an arm around him and say, "Look, that was really a tough situation. You made a good try, you were hustling, and that's what counts. I know what you're going through, but don't worry. I'm behind you."

That's all the coach needs to say. Most youngsters just want to know they are still being supported, and that the coach understands the pressures they are under. But instead we have coaches screaming, "How could you do that? We've been working all week on that play and then you go and blow it. Don't you ever listen? What's the matter with you?" The poor youngster already has his own sense of frustration gnawing away at him, and he knows he's going to have to face his parents. To be scolded and rejected by his coach too leaves him nowhere to turn, except to become further alienated from others, as well as the sport. For people to argue that this kind of toughness builds character is to believe in emotional child abuse.

Dealing with the Potential Superstar

Looking after the top two or three athletes on the team is primarily a matter of all the adults who are involved maintaining the proper perspective. I talked in chapter 10 about how parents must give support and encouragement while also helping the athlete anticipate the pitfalls that can arise. Virtually the same responsibilities lie with the coach. If he recognizes that a child has the physical potential to become an outstanding player as he advances in the sport, then his most important contribution may be to help him mature emotionally.

The coach who has a psychological understanding of the situation will realize that no matter how much talent the youngster might have, and no matter how self-confident he might appear, he is as emotionally vulnerable as anybody on the team. Perhaps more so. He must live up to the high expectations of his parents, which grow with every successful event and heroic moment. He may be driven by his own self-imposed standards and long-term goals. And his teammates are relying on him to help win every game. The coach can never assume that the boy will be able to handle these pressures on his own when things get rough. Thus he should make the athlete aware of the fact that he will have to face these pressures during the season and that people will expect him to produce the big plays week after week, but that he, the coach, won't be expecting these miracles of him. He will be there to support him no matter what happens. After all, even a .300 hitter will fail seven out of ten times.

The coach will add to his own problems in running the team if he gets enamored of his "headline" players. Many coaches, for instance, find they are drawn to the potential superstar more than they are to other members of the team. There is a great personal reward for "discovering" athletic talent, and the coach can bask in the youngster's notoriety. At the same time, however, the youngster may have a disruptive personality. He may have an overbearing ego or he may have difficulty controlling his emotions when things don't go exactly his way, at practice and during the game. Oftentimes the coach will prefer not to notice this behavior or refuse to crack down, fearing his best player will turn against him or go into a sulk. Consequently the youngster and his problems are passed along to the next coach at the next level.

In view of these tendencies, the coach must keep track of his time with the potential superstar to see that it is not excessive, particularly if the individual has numerous personality short-comings. This would suggest that an athlete with personal problems gets more attention, which might encourage others to follow the lead.

The coach also stands to face constant harassment from the immature parents. They will take credit for all the heroics, but if the child is not measuring up to his past performances—or the expectations of the parents—the coach can expect to be accused of poor coaching. Either his approach is wrong, or he doesn't have enough coaching "smarts" to figure out the trouble. (This same mentality prevails at the pro level, where the coach is the first one to be fired when a team starts losing.) The coach's only defense is to deal with the parents on a realistic and factual basis. He must speak in terms of statistical records and objective forms of technical analysis. He cannot allow personal opinions of the youngster to enter into his defense—"Look, you have a rotten kid"—because they will simply use it to further establish their feelings of disrespect for him. If the coach does not represent a mature figure balanced against these parents, the total picture can be one of emotional chaos. When only one parent is immature and offers excuses whenever the youngster makes mistakes, the youngster will always turn to that parent when something goes wrong. The coach then needs to work with the mature parent in order to help keep some balance. In the long run, the athlete will respect the coach for this, but during the process of development it is quite understandable that he will turn to the person who can help him escape pain in time of failure.

The Uncoordinated and Untalented Athlete

There are always those children who show a great deal of interest and boundless energy but who are totally uncoordinated and untalented. These are often the heartbreaking athletes. If they only had the ability, things would be fine. The coach's role in this case is absolutely critical; he can either destroy the last shred of motivation that keeps the child out for the sport or he can make his experience worthwhile and fulfilling. Tennis coach-psychologist Vic Braden explains how the coach at the preadolescent level can have such an impact:

At this point a lot of the athletic talents haven't been identified yet—they are just developing—and a coach should have to accept every youngster. Unfortunately, as a child begins to show special talents the coach forgets good coaching and coaches to the talent. He loves to say, "See that kid dribble to his left? He really has the instinct for basketball." But what about the youngster who has no talent? What about the poor little kid on the bench who has a hard time getting a drink of water without tripping over his feet? He's nothing, absolutely nothing. He's now out of the life of almost every coach. I've known coaches who said, "Forget it, you're never going to make it. You can't hack it. You can't play this game." That's tragic.

What can the coach do who is faced with the youngster who has three thumbs and two left feet, who isn't talented enough to do anything? First of all, the coach must realize that if the child shows up for practices and for games, he's getting something out of it personally, whether it's the attention, learning the sport, or simply belonging to a team. Secondly, the coach can provide a great personal service by trying to give the youngster extra attention. The baseball coach, for instance, might say: "Fenwick, you really seem interested and very eager, so I'll tell you what we can do. If you can come early to the next practice, we'll work on some fundamentals." Then he takes one segment of the game—how to throw the ball properly or how to catch ground balls—and coaches the youngster in a warm, low-keyed manner. Even if Fenwick misses every ground ball, the coach rewards his effort; he doesn't get disgusted and lose his patience. To spread his time, the coach might include three or four of the team's less talented players in these special sessions.

Third, the coach should always be supportive but honest. Don't fool the youngster with false hopes. If he really has no talent, the coach should point out his hard work, dedication, enthusiasm, punctuality, or whatever. He might tell him, "Johnny, I like the way you always hustle. I think that sets a good example for the team. I know that some of the other players are better than you, but you're doing the best you can and I really admire that."

Fourth, the coach who is truly interested in helping to develop better human beings will do all he can to keep the athletic misfit participating in sports. Youngsters who are too heavy, too frail, or too clumsy are the ones who need physical activity the most, yet often the only attention they receive is negative or insensitive. Unless a coach can work with these youngsters to help them conquer their fears and inhibitions about their physical appearance and lack of ability, these youngsters may be lost to sports forever.

What coaching really boils down to is having a respect and concern for each little player on the team. As an example of how sports can provide important benefits to even the lowliest athlete, there was the Little League ball player who was brought to the Child and Family Counseling Services clinic where I teach in San Jose. The boy was ten years old and his problems were already piling up. His father was missing, and his mother was relatively ambitious. She suspected her boy had minimal brain damage or brain dysfunction, because he didn't seem to be very bright. But we discovered there was nothing wrong with his intelligence. We also learned that the boy was an unwanted pregnancy, and unwanted at birth, and that the mother had hostile feelings toward men. Very frequently, for instance, the boy would be put down by his mother just for being a boy.

Fortunately there was a single saving grace—the boy loved Little League baseball. That was all he dreamed about, even though he was an incredibly bad player. He could barely throw, barely catch, couldn't hit, and was a slow runner. But Little League held him together. It provided psychological survival. In fact, the boy would come to the clinic wearing his baseball hat and jersey, and all the counseling would take place while he played catch with the therapist in the little play-ground behind the clinic. We soon learned that the whole concept behind sports was meeting this boy's needs: (1) It allowed him sociability. He was with other boys and he had buddies on the team. (2) There was a male authority figure—the coach—who was concerned about him and who didn't put him down for having a little boy's aggressiveness. (3) It provided a mark of masculinity. He was playing something that other boys played, even though he wasn't very good. (4) He belonged to a team and could wear a uniform.

This case had a strong impact on me, because I realized that by the usual criteria of what made a good ball player—and by the usual screening process—it was clear that this youngster would have been either dropped from the team or completely ignored by the coach. But the boy was lucky. The rules wouldn't allow a player to be cut from a team, and he had a good coach who didn't cringe when he first saw the boy practice. Instead he had the patience to try and help him improve. Little did the coach realize, however, that if baseball had been taken away from this youngster, he would have withdrawn to the point where he actually would have appeared somewhat retarded. What kills me, therefore, is to listen to coaches and parents talk about championships, trophies, records, and all-star teams, as though these were the ultimate contributions and rewards of childhood sports.

The Substitute

I talked earlier about the psychological troubles that beset the bench warmer at all levels of sport: frustration, alienation, futility, and a loss of self-confidence. Given these emotional factors at work on his team, the coach obviously needs to work harder with his substitutes than with his starters in maintaining interest and enthusiasm. Many team coaches have a motto that the test of their team—and their coaching—is whether the last substitute has good morale. If he has, it means everybody has. Yet how does the coach maintain this motivation among players who seldom get to play? In much the same way that he works with the least talented players on the team. He makes it clear that he cares about each of his athletes, no matter what position they play or how far down the bench they might be. Even the lowliest scrub on the team will feel that the coach is concerned about how he is progressing toward his *potential*, not about whether he is winning or contributing directly to a victory. The coach will try to make practice fun for everybody and will never use the benchwarmers as fodder for the first team, nor identify the scrubs as a separate and basically useless wing of the team.

Even though my own participation in sports began back in the 1940s, the philosophy held by my high school basketball coach still holds true today. I grew up in the little town of Gallitzin, Pennsylvania, where my father was a coal miner. As a youngster I was an aimless troublemaker. I had no real goals, nothing that motivated me until I was turned on to basketball by a marvelous coach named Guy Monica. He would open up the gym on Saturday to everybody who wanted to play, and we would choose up sides and play for hours. Monica didn't set up leagues and he wasn't trying to screen players and channel them towards his high school team. He just wanted us to have fun. But he really got us hooked on the sport. I even went into the woods to cut down a pole so I could have support for a backboard; then I worked in the graveyard until I had enough money to buy a basketball. When I eventually made the high school team I was basically a substitute, but Monica did a phenomenal amount for me. He was a hard-driven man, insane about basketball, but he was also extremely supportive. He gave me an identity when, for the most part, I didn't have one. Periodically he would take me aside and say, "I know it's hard being on the bench. It's embarrassing. But I want you to know that I'm very aware of the contribution you're making to the team. It takes a lot of guts to come off the bench. Sometimes you're cold, you're not ready to play, and I know you're hurt by it. But I want you to know that I'm aware of it."

Heck, just that little bit of encouragement, that propping up of my ego, would keep me going for two or three more games. I didn't mind all the bad times sitting on the bench. In fact, I probably worked harder than most of the players, because the coach gave me the feeling that if I really applied myself I could contribute to the team, and I didn't want to let him down. The coach who can instill this feeling in *all* of his players is not only building a strong foundation for team unity, but more importantly, he's working to ensure that each player gains as much enjoyment and self-respect as possible from an involvement in sports.

The Late Bloomer

The coach should be alert to any athlete who has a growth spurt or who progresses rather quickly after seeming to possess little talent. The growth spurt, of course, is not likely to be encountered by the preadolescent coach, but if he can instill a strong, positive experience in the athlete when he is small and generally overlooked, the athlete will make a healthier adjustment to his new physique. A Little League coach in Philadelphia points out: "Why do we have to destroy a little ten-year-old with the idea that if he can't play well, something's wrong with him, when once he's fourteen he might bloom into a hell of a ballplayer?"

For example, I had a friend whose boy played junior high basketball one year. The youngster sat on the bench and rarely played. He was so short and untalented, in fact, that he was nearly cut from the team. But that summer he grew five inches and the next season he was one of the biggest players on the team. Alas, the growth simply produced new problems rather than bringing about instant success. Physically, incredible expectations were made of the boy because of his size, yet he was now awkward and uncoordinated. Psychologically, meanwhile, he hadn't adjusted to his newfound height; his body had grown but not his head. He was given a chance to play, but in critical situations he would revert back to his lack of confidence of a year earlier. The boy's coach was slow to recognize what was happening and only contributed to the problem by expecting the boy's ability to match his size. Fortunately the father was a sensitive person and supported his son all the way through his transition. The boy continued to participate and was gradually gaining confidence and ability as he went into high school.

Before the growth spurt ever comes, or the unexpected jump in ability, a coach can play a crucial role by making the athlete feel good about himself despite his lack of talent or his diminutive size. If the boy knows that his coach really backed him during a tough spot, this feeling will carry over and a positive attitude will continue with the new growth.

Handling Losing

One negative quality that plagues childhood sports is the inability by some coaches to respond to a loss or a losing season in a mature fashion. Their model is Lombardi—"Winning is everything"—and defeat is never to be taken lightly. Laughing is for winners; the losing ball club hasn't earned the privilege. Defeat is even seen as a reflection of the coach personally, as if he as an individual has failed, as well as his players. A coach like this treats losing as a personal affront, glaring at his players with a face that says, "*Why* did you do this to me? What have you got against me?" The same coach will rip into the ten-year-old halfback who fumbles the ball to kill a key touchdown. "Why didn't you hang onto the ball?" he will scream. But his real message is "You're making me look bad as a coach." The sad part is that the athlete wants to win as much as the coach. It just happened that he failed at that time, or the team lost. He certainly didn't volunteer to be a "goat."

The coach who can take losing and make it productive, and still be supportive, is a rare individual. Nobody *likes* to lose, but the rare coach will have his players enjoying competition, just taking part, even if they lose week after week. He does this by taking the focus away from the final score and striving for improvement in each one of his players. At practice, instead of working the team harder and harder with each succeeding loss, he devises little games to lighten the drudgery. His players learn to enjoy the sport, because they are improving as individuals, if not as a team. And should there be a victory or two—even one out of every ten games—the coach will join his players in their excitement; he won't spoil their fun by remarking, "See what you guys could do if you really worked at it? If you didn't make so many bonehead plays you could win every week." And he won't make them feel miserable after the nine losses. It's interesting to note that two of the most successful coaches in history, football's Vince Lombardi and basketball's Red Auerbach, seldom lashed out at their teams after a loss. They knew their players were already down; what they needed was for someone to help bolster their confidence. However, both coaches would criticize in detail after a sloppy win, a tactic that is sometimes effective with consistently winning teams *at the college and professional level*, but hardly recommended for the preadolescent coach. If his goal is to build and maintain a dynasty, using grade school athletes to feed his fantasies, then he doesn't belong in coaching.

I remember meeting my son after a Little League game that his team had won. One of his friends on the losing team came up to him and said, "Darn, I can't go yet. The coach said we have to run around the field ten times 'cause we lost." Imagine going to a game when you're ten years old and having to look forward to that kind of punishment if you lose, when you feel bad enough already. If coaches feel it's necessary for players to run laps, then the *winners* should run them and the losers should get to go and have a Coke. That might promote a better perspective.

When evaluating a coach, one important criterion that parents should use is to judge his team during the last week of the season. If the team is completing a losing season, but the players are showing up for practice and are still enthusiastic— rather than being disheartened and feeling inadequate—and they feel they've gained something personally from the season and are looking forward to playing the following year, then they have a coach who is truly a winner.

14

Building Coach-
Athlete Rapport

THE PREADOLESCENT COACH may lack experience in
the intricacies of coaching, and Dr. Spock may be as far as he
read in child psychology. He might not even have a consuming
drive to build winning teams or winning athletes. But this
doesn't have to be a deterrent to effective coaching. The coach
can be remarkably successful, especially in helping to meet the
emotional needs of his athletes, simply by devoting himself to
the humanistic aspects of sports—personal concern for all his
athletes, sensitivity to emotions, fairness, open communication,
and positive motivation.

Professional athletes will tell you, "Sure the team's important, but first comes me." The preadolescent coach, if he is to
make a healthy contribution, must reverse that philosophy, and
shove his own ego aside. His goal should be to take youngsters
and find out who they are and what they want to achieve, and
then give them a chance to grow as persons, using athletics as a
way of getting there. This character-building *potential* of
sports will be explored in this chapter, and I will suggest steps

189

that can be taken in pursuit of the elusive, yet crucial, rapport among the coach, his athletes, and their parents.

Communication

Just as effective communication within the family is vital to successful child rearing, a key ingredient in preadolescent sports is the coach's ability to communicate with his athletes and their parents. Following are some ways that this interaction can take place.

The coach should invite his athletes and their parents to his house one afternoon for punch and cookies or a hot dog roast. Everybody can relate in an informal setting, and the coach can begin to break down the authoritarian image that inhibits youngsters when they are first getting into sports. The idea, as I pointed out earlier, is for the athletes to see their coach as a firm but friendly uncle, not as an enemy. The coach will also use this opportunity to talk about the season ahead, his goals, and his philosophy about coaching and competition.

The coach should make an attempt to visit the home of every athlete, if only to stay long enough for a cup of coffee. He can meet the parents and the brothers and sisters and learn a little about the family and it's environment. The athlete who is an only child and whose father is a bank president will undoubtedly have a different perspective on athletics and coaches than the sixth child in a family of eight where the father is a truck driver. The coach will try to sense if there are athletes or ex-athletes in the family who are pressuring the youngster to make his mark in sports. The athletically involved family will certainly place greater pressures on a child than the parents who have little, if any, interest in the "fun and games" of their children. Of course, many young athletes thrive on growing up around older brothers and their friends. In most cases, if they are competitive by nature, they take to sports naturally and quickly learn to fend for themselves, and when they cruise into organized sports, they are armed with self-confidence and ability.

The concerned coach will try to have a personal meeting with each athlete. The purpose will not be to lay down the law about rules, practices, and commitments, but simply to become better acquainted. They could talk about the youngster's school, his hobbies or special interests, his athletic heroes, or his favorite teams. The coach should determine why the youngster is participating in sports and how his parents feel about it. Was there a family dispute? What has been his previous experience in sports? Was it fun? What did he like about the sport? Most coaches assume—since they themselves are generally in athletics for this reason—that the athlete enjoys participation and is voluntarily giving up his time to sports. This assumption is made but very often he is participating for other reasons. He may just want the fellowship, he may see sports as a way to gain recognition or a feeling of adequacy (masculinity), or he may be doing it to gain the love and attention of a father who never made it past the minor leagues—in which case the youngster may be rebellious against the coach, rather than his father.

The youngster should also be encouraged to talk about the emotional aspects of sports—pressure, competing for a starting job, the relative importance of winning. For instance, has he had much experience playing under pressure? Does he like all that responsibility on his shoulders, or does it make him too nervous? The coach should empathize with the youngster about pressure and assure him that he will always be there to offer support—never to browbeat—should the child fail in a pressure situation. Perhaps the coach will recall the time he cost his old high school team a championship by missing two free throws with two seconds left, but how the sun still came up the next morning.

A good freewheeling, give-and-take discussion will provide an excellent opportunity for an exchange of confidences between the coach and athlete. It can be their first step towards establishing trust, even though it will be some time before the athlete genuinely believes his voice is being heard. Needless to say, any coach who would use information he obtains in this way *against* the athlete is not only unethical, but he is undermining his profession. If, for example, the athlete confides that he is failing in school, it would be disastrous for the coach to point out during practice, in front of teammates, that the boy is a failure on the field, too.

Once the season is under way, the coach should provide several avenues for feedback from his athletes, since he may be evaluated by his players very differently from the way he views himself. One method is regular team meetings, where the athletes are encouraged to raise any questions, doubts, or complaints about the team and to evaluate the coach—with no threat of punishment if they say something he doesn't like. The coach should have enough confidence in himself to be able to tell his team, "Okay, you guys have taken a lot of guff from me this week; now here's your chance. What did we do this week that you thought was good, and what did you think was bad? When I criticized Fenwick in front of the team, do you think I was fair? Or unfair? Am I doing anything during a game that really bothers some of you, but nobody ever says anything?" The coach who allows himself to be evaluated makes it easier for the athletes to accept evaluation. Even more important is the message that he is making an active effort to communicate.

Some high school coaches ask their players to fill out an evaluation questionnaire at the end of the year, asking for their judgments on the merits of his coaching and suggestions for improvement the following year. The coach shouldn't expect younger players to fill out such a questionnaire, but he should allow them at least a voice in what's going on, because in a real sense it is their team. A better understanding of what is happening from the child's point of view will give the coach a greater empathy with what his athletes are going through.

The coach also needs to communicate his feelings. He should be seen as a human being who is concerned about his players, who goes through his own pain and misery when it comes to deciding who will start and who will sit on the bench and for what period of time. His athletes ought to know that it's not done with great glee. As Vic Braden has said:

I'm a nut about the coach and his athletes meeting together and going through the hard knocks and the triumphs together, so that as the season goes along they understand that the coach is not God, and the sport is not God—that there is something bigger than all this stuff—whether it's the team, the spirit, the sense of unity, the self-image each athlete is getting out of the sport. Whatever it is, it should be a lot bigger than the coach and the sport.

The coach can benefit immensely by an "open door policy," although at the preadolescent level he is unlikely to have a door to lock himself behind, unless he heads straight for his car after practice or a game. The coach should make it clear to his players that if anything is bothering them, they can come to him and he will listen. They must also always feel free to raise a question or express their opinion. The coach who fails to allow this, who inhibits an open exchange of ideas and concerns, is saying, in essence, that the individual is not important and that the coach doesn't have time for him. The coach can hardly expect personal dedication in return.

The coach should also work to maintain communication with the parents during the season and to make them feel more a part of the team. He doesn't have time to talk to every set of parents every couple of weeks; he's not running a child therapy clinic. But with the aid of an assistant coach or a volunteer mother, he could send out a rinky-dink newsletter discussing the team's progress, with positive comments on each athlete. Whenever an incident occurred (positive or negative) that he felt was important to the youngster's growth as an athlete or as a person, he could try to jot down a statement to the parents or tell them in person. This is really all the parents want—some reassurance from the coach that he is watching after their youngster and that he cares enough to keep them informed. In fact, it is possible to view coaching as teaching, where the coach comes up with a "report card" on the youngster's physical and emotional progress: recent improvement, areas that need to be improved, how the parents can help out, and what the coach is trying to do to help the youngster reach his potential. Unfortunately, this could run into the same problem as report cards in school, which are often used as a punishing tool by the parents. Whatever approach the coach takes, the parents should have access to him to discuss their youngster's improvement or any problems that have arisen.

Motivation

One of the most crucial roles played by the coach is that of the motivator. He works with first team athletes who are already successful and makes them want to improve their skills, hopefully through their own self-motivation. Secondly, he nurtures an honest enthusiasm in the bench warmer so that the youngster doesn't develop a negative, complaining attitude that can undermine morale and create factions on the team. A third area is repeatedly brought up by coaches: "How do you motivate youngsters who don't really enjoy being out there— who are playing because of family pressure or who simply want to be with their friends?" Of course, what these coaches are saying is: "Produce some kind of magic so they'll love baseball." But you can't do that. To make youngsters love any sport, the coach has to make it enjoyable *for everybody on the team.* He has to want each of his players to improve while having fun at the same time. He can't tell his athletes, "I assume that all of you are out here because you want to be," and then proceed to run his team like a drill sergeant, forcing everybody through rigorous practices and insisting on a no-nonsense approach. Certainly there's a need for youngsters to learn discipline—things like teamwork, hustling, being on time, trying to perform fundamentals correctly, adhering to an orderly practice. But only as long as the coach gives fair, evenhanded direction, and not when he believes that the only way to become successful is to suffer along the way.

Some coaches, as well as parents, believe that fear is the most effective motivational tool. They feel that children respond best to the fear of punishment, the fear of ridicule, the fear of losing, the fear of losing one's position on the first team. They cloak their philosophy in generalities—"Kids need discipline" —and then proceed to take an incredibly hard-nosed, insulting, no-sympathy "approach" to coaching that can be absolutely damaging to a youngster's self-image. To use fear and intimidation at any stage, or in any area, of child rearing, is wrong. The responsibility of the coach is to kindle a self-sustaining, lifelong interest in participatory athletics, not to drive youngsters away or weed out those who are clumsy and untalented at an early age.

A perfect example of how some adults can lose sight of sports from the child's perspective was presented by the CBS show *60 Minutes* when it focused one week on Pop Warner football in Hollywood, Florida. Commentator Mike Wallace noted that game films were analyzed by the boys, coaches sent plays in from the press box via headset communication, detailed statistics were kept on each play, and four nightly practice sessions were held each week, with a game every Saturday, in a season that stretched from August to December.

The cameras showed the coach of one team, Hollywood Hills, at practice, tearing into a player who had fouled up a play. "What the hell are you doing?" the coach demanded. "We had the same damn thing out of you last night. Every night do I have to chew you out, huh? Every night do I have to get on you?" Meanwhile, another coach tried to inspire the proper frame of mind during "hitting" drills by shouting, repeatedly, "Knock his jock off."

In defense of their tough, professional approach, one coach explained: "We're developing a boy not just physically but mentally, emotionally. All of these things that are taking place in the individual. I think it's going to help him develop for later life. . . . It's competition, you know, they're competing for a position on the team. Later on in life they'll compete for a job."

The program then focused on a key late-season game in which both teams (Hollywood Hills and Miramar) needed to win to keep alive hopes for the play-offs and a shot at the championship. Before the game the Miramar coach solemnly told his players, "We'll beat Hollywood Hills, do you understand?"

"Yes sir!" shouted his players, like squeaky-voiced basic training recruits.

"Get together, gentlemen," the coach continued. "Get together. This is the biggest game in your life."

Meanwhile, the Hollywood Hills coach was exhorting his team to even greater heights. "You want this game?" he asked in the pre-game huddle.

"Yes sir!"

"Are you ready?"

"Yes sir!"

"Are you ready?"

"Yes sir!!"

"ARE YOU READY?!!"

"YES SIR!!" the players screeched at the top of their eleven-year-old lungs.

"Alright, let's go."

At halftime, Hollywood Hills managed to lead, 6–0, but the coach attacked his players as though they were two touchdowns behind in the Super Bowl: "You kids go back out there, you're making this team look better than they are. They stink. I haven't seen anybody stick anybody. We bang all week, two-on-one drills, and you guys don't go out and hit anybody. What are you guys made of? Like a pig farm where I live? Is that what you are? Just stinking pigs? You go out there and show these people what you're made of. I've just about had it with you guys. Spend all this time with you guys and you come out and pull something like this. Catch you standing around. Let's get out of here. Let's go play some football!"

Hollywood Hills proceeded to win, 25–0, and afterwards, with the championship now within reach, the coach could revert to a lovable-guy image. "Good job today," he told his players in the dressing room. "Beautiful. Beautiful job. I love you. You're a great bunch of kids. Let's go celebrate. Let's go celebrate."

Four weeks later, however, Hollywood Hills lost the championship game and finished second. Every player was later presented with a scroll containing some thoughts by Vince Lombardi:

> There is no room for second place. I have finished second twice in my time at Green Bay and I don't ever want to finish second again. There is a second place bowl game but it's a game *for* losers, played *by* losers. It is, and always has been, an American zeal to be first in anything we do, and to win and to win and to win.

Building Character

Many coaches feel that because they work with young people they automatically make a contribution to the character development of each athlete. This faith has become so entrenched that few efforts have been made to determine whether such an assertion is true. In fact, research done by Ogilvie and Tutko would indicate that the coach's assessment of what he is and the actual scores on his personality tests show serious discrepancies. This is particularly true in areas where sensitivity to others is needed. Coaches are not so in tune with the needs and motives of their athletes as they think they are. For example, they feel they look after and nuture others, when in fact they fall short in that need. Coaches must therefore not only evaluate the methods they are employing, but determine *why* they are coaching in the first place. If the coach's answer is, "I'm doing it because I want to help kids," he should think deeper and really explore his motivations. Because in reality, from my own observation and research in the area, many coaches are doing it to fulfill their own needs. They have tunnel vision. Their main concern is to nurture the kids who can make a contribution to winning, and thus to the coach's own ego. They may, in fact, be alienating the very youngsters they think they are helping.

One of my messages to coaches is: Let's be honest. When we talk about the major goal for the season, let's not say it's to build character unless we have a clear-cut program as to how to approach that goal. Let's not say it's helping the players grow and we're doing it for their benefit, if all we do is talk about winning. Only when a coach has a prescribed plan to improve each of his athletes—physically *and* emotionally—can he talk righteously about what he is contributing as their coach.

Earlier I discussed methods by which the coach can establish and maintain communication with his athletes and their parents. Through these discussions, and by his own observations at practice and during the game, the coach will find some specific area—emotional, attitudinal, motivational, or behavioral—where he wants to help each athlete grow as a person. If the child is overly shy, the coach will try to help him learn to speak out and take care of himself; the child who is "flaky" will need to acquire more emotional control; the child who uses aggression to get his way will be rewarded for displays of teamwork and cooperation; the child who has difficulty sticking with a task will be rewarded for working towards specific goals; those youngsters who get easily depressed, the slow learners, or those who just seem lost and befuddled will receive the coach's constant encouragement and even-tempered patience.

The coach will discuss these specific goals with each player so that they understand what he is trying to achieve. The coach shouldn't always expect to succeed; some youngsters are so deeply scarred that they need to have professional help. But as long as the coach is attempting to find ways to get through to his athletes and bring change, he is to be commended. If the coach and the parents can work together and actually help the child strengthen his personality by learning to cope more effectively with the emotions of competition, then sports can make an invaluable contribution to the child's life.

The coach himself should be a model of character development. Rather than just talking, he should exhibit the qualities that he's trying to develop. If he doesn't display these qualities, he can hardly expect his athletes to strive for them. For example, if the coach tries to instill in his athletes the need for staying cool under pressure, and at the same time he's yelling at his players, screaming at the umpires, and threatening fistfights with rival managers, he can hardly expect mature behavior out of his players.

In team sports, as we saw earlier, one telling guideline to good coaching is the attitude of the lowliest bench warmers. If they are having fun and learning something about the sport, then the entire team is likely to have a similar positive attitude. Effective coaching in individual sports can be analyzed in like fashion, as suggested by Vic Braden:

> When I visit tennis clubs the pro always wants me to watch his best players hit the ball. But I ask him to show me the worst ten or fifteen players he has in the whole club. If they've got some idea of how to play, if they enjoy the game, then this coach is worth all the money he can be paid.

A further assurance, at least in the coach's eye, that he has had a healthy influence on his team could simply be a handwritten letter from one of his players, similar to the one received by Steve Urbanovich, the coach of a flag football team for ten- to twelve-year-olds in Burbank, California.

Dear Mr. Urbanovich,

Thank you for coaching us this year and two years ago. You've had a great career as a coach. If we win tonight, your record will be 7–8–1. If we lose, you'll be 6–9–1, and I think that's a great record. I want to thank you for hanging in there this year. There was a lot of horsing around at practice, but you hung in there, even though you might have wanted to do other things. Me, well I've learned a lot from your coaching. Now I'm a much better player. You might want to remember that at your last practice as a coach, Mr. Keltey split his pants. Thanks!!! and we'll miss you!

Sincerely,
Douglas Howe

15

Alternate Models and Approaches

THE "SUCCESS" of childhood sports in this country, in terms of active involvement by millions of young athletes, parents, and coaches, glosses over what I regard as serious shortcomings in our approach to the games children play. Throughout this book I have evaluated many of the myths constructed in defense of highly competitive sports for preadolescents and I have examined the destructive influences of professional and collegiate sports. Now I would like to discuss what I feel are important alternate approaches to winning and competition on the childhood–high school level, including actual programs which have already been successfully implemented here and in Canada.

Philosophical Change

In order for important new directions to be taken, we need a total shift in what parents and coaches value in athletics. We need new mottoes and new goals. Instead of winning (i.e., championships, individual titles, trophies, and medals) being the major justification and reward for sports participation at this level, success in sports should be redefined as "working to your potential." Every young athlete should be judged *only on his own or her own;* they should not be measured in terms of how they do as compared to others. A winner, in my estimation, is the person who works to the best of his ability and involves himself wholeheartedly, even if he loses every time he competes. He enjoys winning but does not have to "win" in order to enjoy the sport. He turns the challenge of sports inward by striving to improve his ability in competition with the standards he has established; he learns, in effect, that improving your tennis game doesn't have to mean beating another person.

A loser, conversely, is one who may very well be "successful," yet is a poor competitor. The youngster who weighs two hundred pounds and plays fullback on the junior high school team is going to be successful on every play. He'll be a hero. But is he really working towards his potential? Is he learning how to block and to catch passes so that he'll be a better all-around player? Does he cooperate with his teammates, or is he a complainer, already seeking special privileges? Does he set a good example in practice by working hard, or is he a pain in the neck to the coaches?

Similarly, what possible benefits are gained by letting a twelve-year-old boy who stands six feet tall and terrorizes the other players with his fastball pitch in Little League? Sure, he might bring glory to himself and his parents by pitching a string of no-hitters, and his team will probably win the league championship. But meanwhile he has made the sport hateful to all the other players. Even his teammates are bored to death, yawning at endless strikeouts and waiting for the one or two balls that might be hit their way during the game. Oftentimes the only exercise the outfielders get is running back and forth to the dugout. The ultimate tragedy, as we saw earlier in the chapter on injuries, is that this youngster is already pitching on borrowed time.

So why have the boy pitch? Just to win ball games? To make the coach and the parents look good? Our competitive ethic leads to the rationale, "Well, he's our best pitcher and he intimidates every hitter in the league, so we use him as often as we can. Besides, he *wants* to pitch and his teammates want to win." This is where all the adults involved need to replace their thirst for victories with a badly needed perspective and a sense of fair play. They should have the boy learn to play other positions such as shortstop and center field (in most cases he is already one of the best athletes on the team) and concentrate on improving his hitting and running skills. Not only will he save his arm for high school, when he will have plenty of time to hone his pitching ability, but he may display unusual ability at a position offering greater longevity.

Another diseased obsession that needs to be rooted out—at all levels of sport—is our total absorption in "Who won?" In a sport like tennis, for example, hundreds of thousands of youngsters will play a match on a given Saturday, and half of them will lose. But when they go home, their parents invariably ask the wrong question—"Did you win?" instead of "Did you have fun? What shots were working best? Did you try anything new? Was it a good match?" We are so consumed by final scores and statistical achievements that the expressed meaning of sport often gets lost in the shuffle, i.e., that it's not whether you win or lose, but how you play the game. In fact, this motto is often thrown back at losers as a measure of belittlement or ridicule. To profess a belief in this ideal is obviously to lack the necessary "killer instinct" that carries one to the top, because competitive sports are "ruthless" and nobody has much sympathy for the "good loser."

We have such an imbedded belief that the winner must be a cut-throat competitor that when a winner comes along, like Evonne Goolagong Cawley, who professes, "Winning is just not everything," even her opponents get a little shook up. "She's infuriating to play against," said England's Virginia Wade. "Always smiling whether she's winning or losing. You get the feeling she just doesn't give a damn, and it throws you off." Even after Goolagong was Wimbledon and Forest Hills champion, her coach, Vic Edwards, said: "I don't think Evonne is a real pro yet. She plays the game because she loves it, whereas a pro tries to win all the time. I don't mean that Evonne *doesn't* try to win, but it doesn't worry her very much if she doesn't."

Charles Schulz, who chronicles the athletic adventures of Charley Brown and friends, is among the outspoken critics of this American preoccupation with winning. He argues that our prime interest, as spectators and as parents, should be to enjoy the quality of performance, not the result:

No sooner does the season start than we begin to record how far a team is out of first place. A game between two teams in 7th and 10th place can be just as exciting as any game. But all we're worrying about is who wins. It should be the plays, great goals being scored, great baskets being made, great overhand shots hit. These are the things that count in sports.

They don't even have to be great plays. It's the flow of the game, the strategy, the unexpected twists, the errors, and the bad breaks that provide a sustaining interest for the discerning spectator.

From the athlete's point of view, the underlying competitive ethic for childhood sports should be an emphasis on the sheer enjoyment of participating in a sport and striving for self-improvement, even if "victory" is never achieved. You compete, but winning and losing are not an expression of personal success or failure. One measurement can be the athlete's consistency over the season, or a marked improvement from the first game to the last. In sports like gymnastics, diving, and figure skating, where perfection is never fully achieved even by Olympic champions, the quest can be the artistry of a creative expression. As Billie Jean King once said: "Tennis has made my life. Winning isn't the big deal, either. The real joy comes from the very thing that involved people in sport in the first place—the fun of execution, the fun of playing." A similar viewpoint was expressed by football coach Joe Paterno when he gave the Penn State commencement address in 1973: "We set high goals for our people. My squad even has to listen to me quote Browning, who said: 'A man's reach should exceed his grasp or what's a Heaven for?' We strive to be No. 1. . . . But win or lose, it is the competition which gives us pleasure."

Instead of Win at all costs, we need a dictum such as Sportsmanship at all costs. Athletes like Arthur Ashe, Jack Nicklaus, O. J. Simpson, and John Havlicek have proven that intense competitors can push to the limits and, win or lose, still be gracious people. Keeping winning in perspective doesn't mean that we don't *strive* to win. As Robert Creamer wrote in *Sports Illustrated*:

The often misunderstood Olympic concept of "taking part" is fully as important as the belief in winning. "Taking part" means trying to win, and trying to win is as vital to sport as winning. Maybe more so. Winning is what you want to do, and what you try your absolute best to do—because if you don't try, if you don't really take part, you cheat yourself and you cheat your opponent and you cheat your sport.

If parents are unable to cut themselves loose from the winning craze, they can hardly expect their children to. Until recent years, in fact, it never occurred to most people involved in sports to look for alternatives to winning. Yet once they think in terms of seeing value in an honest, all-out effort—regardless of whether they are the big winner in the end—they sort of like the idea. The key is for them to retain this perspective when their children are competing. They need to remember the attitude expressed by Sean, a seven-year-old competitor in an all-comers track meet in Eugene, Oregon. As

reported by Bobbie Moore in *Sports Illustrated*, the little boy
proclaimed, "I got fourth-place ribbon yesterday in the 220!"

"Terrific! How fast did you run?" An adult asked.

"As fast as I could," the youngster replied.

Actually, there may be a large, untapped resentment against
the emphasis on winning in this country, as Dr. Ray Canning
sensed from a "pedantic little study" he conducted on handball
players at the University of Utah. Dr. Canning had one group
of players choose their partners for doubles competition where
the emphasis was on competition and winning. Scores were
posted, won-lost records were charted, and trophies were
promised to the winners. The other group stressed cooperation, enjoying the class, and helping each other. The results
were not unexpected. The players in the competitive group
tended to choose partners who would help them win the game,
while those in the cooperative group chose partners on a
random basis. What *did* surprise Dr. Canning, when the
results of the study were made public, was that he received
countless phone calls from people who "agreed" with him that
there is too much emphasis on winning in sports. Some even
called him a "soul brother."

The Coach's Role

Alternate approaches to winning and competition will obviously flounder without a corresponding change in attitude by
coaches. If we eliminated all the coaches in the world today,
the exact same type would replace them. This is particularly
true on the professional, collegiate, and high school levels. It
would take a revolutionary overhaul of sports for significant
new approaches to emerge. Our research at San Jose, for
example, has shown that coaches are aggressive, self-assertive,
and highly organized, and have fierce psychological endurance.
But they are also inflexible in their profession as coaches; they
dislike change and experimentation; and they are extremely
conservative politically, socially, and attitudinally. In addition,

many coaches just can't envision getting joy out of sports outside the cultural expectation of winning. Their basic goal in sports—either through training or their experiences as an athlete—has been primarily focused on winning. Winning brings satisfaction, recognition, and a chance to move up to a better coaching opportunity. So when somebody asks a coach, "Is winning all that worthwhile?" they threaten his basic value structure. Such questioning denies his life's work, in many cases. One can see slight changes on the horizon, however, with coaches more concerned about athletes than about victories.

Fortunately, in this regard, most preadolescent coaches come from a different mold than their full-time counterparts on the high school–college–professional level, thus allowing hope for an eventual cooling of the competitive ethic at the grass roots level. Many of these youth coaches are simply fathers. They may have differing temperaments and political viewpoints, but one attribute they nearly all share is that they're conscientious. They wouldn't spend their evenings and weekends working with children if they weren't. Furthermore, in most cases they want to do what is right. The problem, as we have seen, is that they are as untrained in child psychology as they are in coaching techniques, and thus they all too often turn to the most visible model—the professional or collegiate coach—when in fact they should be operating under entirely different guidelines and motivations.

At this level, therefore, encouraging the coach to adopt a more humanistic approach to winning, competition, and individual participation is primarily a matter of time and training. Viewed in terms of the alternate model, the "winning" coach should be defined as one who helps each athlete work toward his or her maximum potential, regardless of physical ability or mental quickness. The coach is abusing his power and responsibility if he concentrates solely on his best players in pursuit of a league championship, if he drives youngsters away from the sport by burning them out from overwork and too much intense competition, or if he destroys the motivation of those who ride the bench by treating them like losers.

Instead, the coach should strive to help each of his athletes become psychologically more mature and ready for teenage life as a result of participating in sports. I'm convinced that a coach at the preadolescent level can have a totally losing season, but because of his attitude and the way he works with his players, everyone nevertheless ends up feeling good. They all enjoy the sport and can joke about their losses, while looking forward to the next season. It takes a lot of preparation on the coach's part and a great deal of concern for the individual youngster to achieve this feeling. But this is the direction in which coaching must move. The hard-nosed coaches can maintain their competitiveness, but in the context of valuing an honest, all-out effort regardless of whether they win in the end. They should be educated to these other goals and the rewards that aren't necessarily reflected in the won-lost column. They should realize that many fine, unsung coaches gain their deepest self-satisfaction from seeing the growth that takes place in the individual athlete over the season, or even in a single game.

One way the coach can implement the alternate model is to tackle specific personality problems or deficiencies in each athlete, as I discussed in chapter 13. He might say to himself, "Fenwick always gets intimidated. Everybody always pushes him around. I'm going to help him learn to stand up and assert himself—on and off the court. Fred gets so nervous that it causes him to make a lot of mistakes. I'm going to try to help him gain emotional control through sports. Clyde seems to be afraid to set any goals and work towards them. I'm going to help him establish realistic goals and reward him when he achieves each one." As the season moves along, if Fenwick finally starts asserting himself on the basketball court, the coach will make a point of praising him in front of the whole team. In the dressing room after a game he might say, "I want everybody to know that in my estimation the most important change today occurred in Fenwick. He went into the game when he was cold but he made two terrific passes, he scored three baskets, he stole the ball, and he didn't let his man score a point. He really showed he could handle himself out there."

This is what coaches should be working towards. Forget the final score; winning is a very fleeting, temporary sensation. But one player—Fenwick—was a more confident person because he played well under pressure, and the coach noticed it and pointed it out to his temmates. By tackling these tangible psychological characteristics in each athlete, the coach can gain genuine satisfaction from his job, no matter whether his team wins or loses. This is the real joy and reward of sport, because the game and the season are soon forgotten, but each young athlete has a lifetime ahead of him.

The coach who is applying the alternate model, when asked what his goals are for the season, might reply, "We have fifteen different goals this year—one for each player. And I'm working at saying nice things to my players, because I usually yell at them." Even if he has a lousy team, talent-wise, he will establish goals for the season. He will work to have his athletes enjoy the sport and help them maintain a sense of confidence and worthwhileness despite unending defeats.

To be effective, this alternate approach to coaching needs the backing of parents as well as league and sports officials. They all need to realize that the coach's main responsibility is to aid in the physical and emotional growth of each athlete. Those parents and officials who judge a coach's "effectiveness" by his won-lost record or by the number of champions he produces have totally misguided value structures. The truth of the matter is that the championship coach may have been the poorest coach in the league in terms of interpersonal relationships. He may have driven and cajoled his players to the point of winning, but in a totally negative, hostile manner.

One way youth leagues can improve the perspective of their

coaches is to organize preseason seminars or clinics that deal with the emotional and psychological aspects of childhood sports. Speakers could include teachers who work with preadolescents, child psychologists, and physical educators from a local high school or university. Such a panel could also be expanded to include a local doctor or sports trainer with knowledge of the injuries common to the sport.

League officials also need to insure that coaches have a tolerant climate in which to change their competitive approach. Sure it's nice to have winning teams, as long as no one is left out in the process. Sure there's a need for personal challenge and risk-taking, to have youngsters test their physical abilities and potential—but not when the penalties for failure are so high.

Instead of organizing leagues to develop and promote the talented youngster, the goal should be to have athletic programs that are "developmental and instructional up until the teens," suggests Gale E. Mikles, the physical educator from Michigan State. "Let's not make our programs so damn serious and so damn restrictive and elite that all the kids don't have a chance to get in and play, because many of these youngsters are late developers. They're not going to come on early and look great, and you're going to lose them. A lot of good kids just get wasted before they get a chance."

If parents especially can de-emphasize their push and their emphasis on winning, the coaches will find a much more tolerant climate in which to change their approach. Fortunately, many coaches, league officials, and physical educators have implemented interesting new approaches around the country which emphasize positive techniques and a healthy approach to competition. Although some of the ideas are being attempted at the high school level, they could easily be adapted to preadolescent sports. Coincidentally, many of these people also have successful records. But I'm not trying to sell victories; they're peripheral to the philosophy I'm advocating. The first concern must always be the young athlete. Here are some examples of individuals and programs that provide alternate models:

1. From 1960 until his retirement in 1974, football coach George Davis allowed his players to vote on the starting lineup before every game, an exhilarating exercise in democracy that until recent years was virtually ignored—even condemned—by his coaching brethren. Not that Davis wasn't successful—his teams once won a state record 45 straight games at St. Helena High in Sacramento—but he threatened many of the coaches in his field by rejecting what had become their prerogative: absolute, unchallenged authority.

Davis coached his last five years of football at Willits High, California, where today he is the wrestling coach. His players would vote every Wednesday on the starters for Friday's game, allowing for a Thursday practice to work together as a team in case new starters were voted in since the previous game. The players would mark secret ballots that listed all the players at their respective positions. Davis would indicate his preferred starting lineup but would abide by however the players voted. If the vote was close at a particular position, the two players would split the playing time. "Coaches don't think there is enough good in the kid to trust him," said Davis, a soft-spoken, reflective type. "But 90 percent of the time the players select the same ones to start in a game that I would."

A former center and linebacker at Southern Cal, Davis believes a humanistic approach eliminates such traditional coaching problems as training rules violations ("They know if they don't put out, they won't get elected.").

"I also didn't have to explain to parents why their son wasn't starting. As soon as the player recognized his self-interest, it became his strongest motivational factor, and the strength of the peer group made me prepare much more for my responsibilities."

At first, Davis had trouble selling his program to the players (and parents) in Willits, a small, conservative lumber town.

His team lost its first three games while the experiment was going on and he began to receive letters, phone calls, and threats which questioned such participatory ideals. "But once the players began to believe in themselves," said Davis, "we ended up tying for the league championship." The following year, however, his team slumped to a 2–7 season. "They voted for their buddies and for guys who missed practices. They had no leader among them. So you know what happened? They lost. And you know what? They deserved it. I don't think anything could have changed them. School is preparation for life and football is part of school."

Davis feels that allowing youngsters to handle responsibility in this manner makes better citizens of them, and also better football players:

> You have to give kids a chance to make mistakes so they can find out what the problems are. It gets them involved, committed, which is very important today. In practice they are more alert and they concentrate more. They are learning about the entire team, not just one position. They learn to appreciate the decisions the coach has to make and it teaches them to make the decisions that they have to make in the game. In the final analysis the game will depend on their decisions.
>
> The coach's job is to foster ability, but even more to get out of the way of it. Too many coaches get in the way of the free, spontaneous explosion of ability that lies within kids. Many people, not only coaches, feel that the human animal is better motivated by fear than by your belief in them. I have faith in my boys' ability.

I think it's tragic that in a country supposedly based on democracy, many of our most prominent coaches are dictators —Woody Hayes, Vince Lombardi, Bear Bryant, etc.—while a man like George Davis, who practiced democracy, was considered aberrant, "a dangerous radical." He was putting into practice, in a miniature society, the true concept of democracy. The players who received the most votes were going to represent their teammates out on the field. They didn't want to let the voters down. If they didn't hustle, if they goofed around, or if the other player at their position was performing better at practice, their "constituency" would provide instant feedback. What better way to instill a sense of democracy in teenagers? Yet everywhere, at all levels of sport, the majority of coaches insist on being the one-and-only power, the unquestioned dominant figure.

2. The democratic approach can be equally successful in basketball, as Jerry Krause is proving at Eastern Washington State College. Head coach Krause has developed what he calls "a complete program of shared responsibility," beginning in the fall when the players determine the basic rules regarding training, conduct, and appearance, and how they will be enforced. Once the season begins, Krause sets up practices so that those who are in his view the top eight or nine players work together for the first three days of the week. Then two days before the weekend games, the players vote on the starting lineup. Krause can change the lineup for the second game in a weekend series, but he rarely uses this prerogative.

During the game itself, the players determine most of the substitutions. "I want each guy going all-out for four or five minutes," says Krause. "When he's tired he just raises a hand and I send in a substitute. Then when he's had a breather he goes back in. This eliminates pacing, and helps each player work toward playing up to his potential. If they play just for the coach, they're afraid to extend themselves; they play just hard enough to stay ahead of the coach's substitution."

Krause, a coach since 1966, first implemented his program in 1972, and has had winning teams. "But," he points out, "that's not the important thing. We've redefined success as approaching your potential both as a player and a person. Our coaches and players feel much better about our program and about athletics. In fact, our morale and competitiveness have been better than any time in my coaching career. It's just fun to go into the gym for practice every day. The guys are in there early and they stay late, working on their own. They're much more concerned now with earning the respect of their teammates."

One value of having the players vote on the starting lineups, Krause points out, is that there are things that happen to an individual—in the locker room or in his personal life—that the coach may be unaware of but not his teammates. For example, early in the 1974 season the team captain was voted out of the starting lineup. "That kind of shook me up," Krause admits. "We had a young team and I wanted my experienced players in there as a steadying influence, especially on the road. But the captain was having personal problems and not practicing very hard, and his teammates voted him out. We lost that first game and I had the option to start him in the second. But I decided to leave him on the bench. When he got into the game as a substitute, he played one of the best games of his career and ended up having a good senior year."

Although his school, EWC (enrollment 7,000), is not UCLA, Krause says, "I'd love to give my approach a shot at a big college. I'm convinced that in the next ten years you're going to see major teams using a democratic approach, and succeeding."

3. Cartoonist Charles Schulz, who built a $2 million ice hockey–skating rink for himself and the people of Santa Rosa, California, said that one of his motivations stemmed from his negative experiences in the public school system of his childhood. "It didn't cater to the many kids who weren't big and strong. The gym teachers paid attention only to the school athletes. The rest of us were shunted aside. I really resented that." Thus, when he opened his ice rink, he declared "that everybody who signed up was going to get a uniform and play on some kind of team regardless of ability. He wasn't going to sit on the bench—especially in this kind of game, where youngsters are playing and it's supposed to be for fun."

4. Hockey player–coach Pat Stapleton is one professional who retains the sensitivity of his childhood. Speaking of his sideline career as a rink builder and manager, he said: "I made

a rule when we opened the Downers Grove rink [in Chicago] that a buzzer had to go off every two minutes and the coaches had to change their lineups in kids' games. The coaches hated it. They wanted to win. I want the kids, all the kids, to play hockey. Who cares whether you win or lose at the age of seven or eight?"

5. Bob Krolak, the director of the hockey program in Oak Lawn, Illinois, near Chicago, told *Sports Illustrated* writer Mark Mulvoy that "Parents are the kids' worst enemies. They don't do anything except criticize." One night Krolak had a bitter argument with a father who claimed his eight-year-old son did not get enough ice time. "My boy's the best player on the team," the father said, "and he should be playing twice as much as the other kids." When the father walked away, Krolak shook his head. "This man here can't get it through his head that we want recreation, not competition, for these kids. All he cares about is seeing his own score 50 goals. We just try to give them all equal time."

6. The National Junior Tennis League is a rarety among national sports program for youngsters, simply by trying to deemphasize the win-at-all-costs philosophy within its ranks. Organized in 1969 to try to bring the game to urban areas where tennis normally isn't played, the nonprofit league started out with typical American priorities: each member city formed leagues and teams competed within the leagues. Then each league winner competed for the city championship and the city champion then competed in a national championship at Forest Hills. After several years, however, the league organizers realized that had a built-in contradiction. Explained executive director Ray Benton:

When we started out we discovered that the kids wanted the opportunity to play immediately. Forget the basic instruction. Nobody taught them how to dribble a basketball. They picked it up themselves on the playgrounds. Nobody taught them how to bat a ball. They picked it up themselves on the sandlots. They were kids who just wanted to play and have fun.

We wanted as many kids to play as possible, and we didn't emphasize winning, we emphasized development. The system was supposed to be confined to the basics. But we were saying, "Get to be city champs and you may get to Forest Hills."

Finally, in 1975, with over 60 cities and 100,000 kids involved, the league decided not to hold national playoffs. "We realize it's a step opposite to where most sports are heading," said Benton. "But we want kids to learn there's more to tennis than just winning championships. These youngsters are novices (ranging in age from ten to eighteen) with little or no tennis experience. At this level, the desire to win at a site like Forest Hills places too much pressure on them."

7. The YMCA is an active force behind positively run sports programs for children, although their motto "Every boy plays in every game" obviously needs updating, what with their increasing attention to leagues for girls. ("We feel that girls have the same athletic needs as boys," said one YMCA official.) Steve Cassell, director of the Pacific Palisades–Malibu program, talked about the YMCA philosophy:

Our goals are geared to the human touch. We want each child to enjoy participating in a sport with a minimum of pressure, and an emphasis on learning skills while having fun. Our awards system is set up to provide an award for all who participate, and we do not crown league champions. From the opening day, every effort is made to insure that teams and competition remain on an equal level. While winning and losing are a real part of the game, we are more concerned that participants have an experience that will teach them lessons about being a team player.

The Y's flag football program, for instance, tries to insure relatively equal competition by having preseason evaluation clinics where each player is tested in such basic football skills as blocking, passing, evasiveness in running, receiving, punting, speed, and aggressiveness. Coaches rate each youngster on a one to four basis in each skill area, and the teams are then divided up according to these ratings. Later, YMCA staff members observe the first practice games to make sure one team isn't going to steamroll the opposition or that another team is hopelessly outclassed. If these inequalities exist, players are switched around before team identities are really set.

The national YMCA has also formed a basketball league for boys and girls age eight to eighteen, in cooperation with the National Basketball Association Players Association. The purpose is to foster sportsmanship rather than competitiveness by stressing the development of personal values as well as basketball skills and the fun of playing the game. Every child who registers plays in every game and players receive certificates for having participated. Unlike the Little League, there's no pressure to win trophies, make all-star teams, or shoot for national competitions. In fact, the program actively discourages aggressive attitudes while promoting a concern for the less talented players.

8. Basketball in Hobbs, New Mexico, provides a refreshing example of how a "winning" high school program can coexist in a healthy manner with mass participation. Ralph Tasker's Eagles are a perennial power—seven times state champs through 1975—and they play in a manner that maximizes the contributions of all thirteen boys on the team. Tasker's strategy is to employ an aggressive, full-court defense, "the Hobbs press," throughout the game, no matter what the opposing strategy. "Of course, the boys need a rest, so that's why everybody plays in every game," said Tasker. "The boys on the bench know they are going to be playing, so each roots for the boy playing his position and studies his opponent." Tasker also sees that every player starts at least once during the season. (Graduates include Bill Bridges, formerly of the Los Angeles Lakers and former Texas All-American Larry Robinson.) "I don't see how coaches who play only six or seven players the whole game can keep the other players happy," Tasker said.

The town itself is basketball crazy. The gym opens at 7:00

in the morning in the summer, and there are leagues playing until 10:30 at night. Tasker pointed out:

Folks in Hobbs believe that the gym—and the other school facilities—should be left open for the public to enjoy. Evenings, weekends, everything. So these little kids come in and play three-man basketball whenever they feel like it. We feel we should encourage kids to come off the streets. If they can direct all that energy to sports, they can stay out of trouble. We don't coach them. There's just enough supervision to care for the building. But our taxpayers believe that once the gym is built, it ought to be used. No use locking it up and saving it for tomorrow. It's needed now.

This enthusiasm for basketball, even at the grade school level, is reflected when the high school team comes out on the floor for its pregame warm-up. Six mascots, aged eight and nine and dressed in little Eagle uniforms, also take the floor. They go through the warm-up with the varsity and then put on a ball-handling drill of their own, to the music of the student pep band. Many of these mascots later play on the varsity as the cycle keeps feeding itself.

9. Several Little League programs (Menlo Park, California, and Houston among others) have been enjoying notable success by employing a pitching machine in place of the pitcher during games for eight- and nine-year-olds. But why not make it standard equipment for *all* Little League games through age twelve? Tradition—"Don't tamper with the game!"—is the common defense of those who seem to think youngsters enjoy playing a game where there are dozens of walks and strikeouts but few hits and very little real action. Pitching machines (especially one called JUGS) will eliminate these problems while providing numerous other short-term and long-term benefits for the youngsters as well as the sport: (1) JUGS has such excellent control that there is no fear of being hit, and thus the batter learns to stand in there and take his "cuts." He develops the confidence to hit a fastball and a curveball and to bunt. (2) The machine helps expedite practice

by putting the ball over the plate on every pitch, so each batter gets his maximum number of swings. It can also be used to "hit" ground balls to infielders or fly balls to outfielders. (3) During a game, with the machine throwing the ball right down the middle, nobody walks and youngsters learn to hit the ball and run the bases. Defensive fielding plays (ground balls, popups, flies) increase dramatically, and everyone has a chance to learn to play his position. Play speeds up, there's more action, more players come to bat, and there's more to get excited about. As *Sports Illustrated* pointed out: "This way, batting and fielding skills improve tremendously, and pitching does not become important until the kids are older and better equipped to cope with it." However, they can stand next to the machine and learn to field their position, without risking damage to their growing arm.

10. Another suggestion to improve the game at the Little League level would be to have players switch positions every inning or two innings. The right fielder would then have an incentive to learn to play the infield and would get in on the action more often, while the catcher would have a chance to roam centerfield. Switching positions in this manner would also help the coach deal with the parent who complains, "I'm not raising an obscure right fielder—I want a pitcher." By dividing up the pitching, everybody would learn the mechanics of the position while it would take the stress off the throwing arm.

Furthermore, leagues should have a rule that every player must play at least two innings and must get at least one turn at bat every game, no matter how important the game is to the league standings.

11. A highly organized, regimented institution like Pop Warner football desperately needs a change in emphasis. Sure the game is rough, but that doesn't give youth coaches a license to teach hate or viciousness as the key to becoming a good football player, or a winning team. As one high school coach puts it, "I think football is a good thing for kids if it is taught

right, but other things are important—peace, love, honesty, school. I think you can teach good values for life *and* produce a good football team. If I can't do that, then I don't want to coach."

In addition to de-emphasizing a violent approach to the game, youth football leagues need to broaden the playing opportunities for every youngster. Instead of fielding unwieldy thirty-three-man teams, why not have twenty kids on a side and more teams, so that everybody can play at least half a game? If there aren't enough playing fields to accommodate the extra games on Saturday, shrink the playing dimensions so that two games can go on simultaneously instead of one. And if this means fewer coaches for each team, is that really a tragedy? Why not give the kids a chance to run their own affairs? Let them devise their own plays, draw up their own starting line-ups, and work out a system of substitution. The coach and his assistants can be around to provide instruction and emotional support, but once the game begins they should withdraw from the sidelines.

Two other provisions that can guarantee hope for the benchwarmer are: (1) When one team gets ahead by a certain score—say sixteen or twenty points—the coach must take out his starting line-up; and (2) a must-play rule where every player gets to play at least one series every quarter. Says Bob Cupp, who coaches a kids' football team near Palm Beach, Florida:

> The idea is to have fun, period. If a kid isn't, if he's not enjoying it and quits, the coach should ask himself, "Would he have quit if I'd done a better job?" [Kids] should be playing more and practicing less, anyway—playing three or four games a week instead of seven or eight a season. Practicing one-on-one, hitting dummies—that's a drag. A kid wants to play. Lord knows, he's going to find less time for it later on.

Cupp and his "revolutionary" ideas about kids' football were featured in a provocative 1975 *Sports Illustrated* story by John Underwood, titled appropriately, "Taking the Fun Out of a

Game." Cupp's most radical approach to the game is a rotation system which insures that each player, in every game, gets to play a position in which he actually handles the ball. Each youngster is given at least one shot at a ball-handling position (quarterback, halfback, fullback, or receiver) but everybody must also take a turn as an interior lineman. Cupp recalls that interesting things happened when he first implemented his system:

The parents objected, some of them. Some of the kids objected, too. One kid refused to play anything but center. He said he didn't want to goof up. But after a while even the prima donnas came to realize there was more to football than being the star and everybody else blocking. . . . The thing is, it was fun for the kids, and fun for me. I can't tell you the kick I get seeing a kid discover the joys of football. . . . I used to see stagnation set in when kids were relegated to a position like guard or tackle for the whole year. It was like a sentence. Before long, many of the linemen wouldn't even show up for practice. They were usually the smallest guys, anyway—that's the way it works in the little leagues—and what did they need with extra punishment? They were getting enough on Saturday. I couldn't blame them. . . . Let's face it. Running the ball, throwing it, catching a pass, making touchdowns—those are the things kids think of as football. Sustained drives and quality blocking they may think about later, when they're in high school, but for now they don't and shouldn't have to. We're not a feeder system for the high school coaches.

What We Can Learn From Junior Hockey in Canada

Amateur hockey in Canada, which entices youngsters into the system as young as six and rejects over 99 percent of them before they reach the professional ranks, has all the fanaticism and neurosis of American youth sports rolled into one patriotic package. "More than any language, race, custom, flag or anthem, hockey is the Canadian common denominator," wrote William R. McMurtry in his provocative report on the state of the sport in Canada ("Investigation and Inquiry into Violence in Amateur Hockey"). "Hockey is of desperate importance to many of our youth," he said, "and the effect of his experiences in sport may have a far more profound influence on his character and attitudes than any part of his academic education."

In view of hockey's impact, the fact that junior hockey has grown so blatantly commercial, competitive, and violent in recent years—following the lead of the professionals—has led concerned Canadians to counterattack. Physical educators, recreation directors, parents, and coaches are all trying to implement new competitive approaches, especially for youngsters under fourteen. Many of their ideas would be a healthy antidote for our own junior hockey programs.

Philosophically, attempts are being made to educate hockey hardliners and those who are beginning to waver—coaches and parents alike—that amateur hockey has a purpose greater than to train professionals. On the younger levels especially, fun, recreation, and the development of skills must take precedence over winning games and championships.

For example, the Sports Institute for Research at the University of Windsor, Ontario, has devised a project that features no-win games in an organized league structure. According to Dr. James Duthie, "the sport is being returned to the children" by taking the competitive aspect out of it. No points are awarded for won or lost, no goals are counted, and there are no records of leading scorers. The league had twenty-eight teams in a recent season, and the youngsters seemed to have a lot of fun. There was a reduction in aggression and violence during play, and less sadness afterwards.

Physical educators at the University of Alberta have also made efforts to switch the focus away from winning and elitism, where the talented players get most of the playing time and coaching attention while the others sit on the bench. An alternative league was set up in Edmonton that put the emphasis on instruction and participation by every player, regardless of ability. Instead of one game being played the full length of the ice, three games were played simultaneously across the rink. Each team had only six players and a goalie and they were all on the ice for the entire one-hour game, instead of playing in two-minute shifts for a total playing time of about twenty minutes.

Every youngster played every position, so that the fat kid in goal could take his turn out on the ice while the hot-shot scorer would learn what the goalie had to put up with. The coaches were called instructors and they would skate on the ice with the players. Thus they could provide on-the-spot instruction, or could stop the game to talk about strategy while the players caught their breath.

"At first, this program had tremendous opposition from people in the community," said Dr. Richard Alderman, a physical educator at the University of Alberta. "There wasn't the traditional competition with teams from outside the area, and the parents wanted their kids to play hockey on a regulation rink. It's true that a youngster is going to learn to skate better on a bigger ice surface, but this can come when they're thirteen or fourteen." Meanwhile, by playing constantly for almost a full hour, youngsters in this alternative league were learning better hockey skills at a faster rate and having a lot more fun. For example, because of the closer quarters every player handled the puck much more often than in a traditional game.

"By the middle of the season everyone was all for our program," said Alderman, "except the coach of the big community team. He even tried to steal some of our players, but the parents wouldn't let their kids shift. They knew their kids were learning more hockey skills."

Another goal of the hockey reformers in Canada is to somehow stem the unwarranted violence that is marring an otherwise elegant game. They are trying to counteract the professional model by stressing that there is nothing gallant about fighting, even if the crowd loves it and tradition says it's the manly thing to do. They also contend that a contact sport need not, in itself, be violent. Wrote William R. McMurtry: "Seldom if ever does an athlete resent a body check within the rules. In fact most relish it, whether on the giving or receiving end. It is usually when the parents and coaches emphasize retaliation and 'getting even' that contact sport degenerates into violence." McMurtry also pointed out that the more skill a boy develops, the less reliance he will place on aggression and violence.

Not only in Canada but in the United States, we need a philosophical change by coaches and parents—and young players—away from a belief in the so-called virtues of fighting and intimidation. Instead of condoning violence as "part of the game," why not try to curb it with strict enforcement of sensible rules for "the good of the game"? In Toronto, for example, fighting and verbal abuse of the officials has been virtually eliminated in junior hockey by the enforcement of rules calling for ejection from the game and an appearance before the league board. And it's interesting to note that Russian hockey schools for young boys stress conditioning and expertise, not body contact or fighting. Youngsters are actually forbidden to body-check for the first seven or eight years of their play in little leagues, and yet the Russians certainly develop world-class hockey teams.

An Alternate Sport—Soccer

Given their choice, thousands of American youth are rejecting the regimentation and violence of Pop Warner football and turning to soccer, a sport that offers constant action and involvement, relative safety, and far less emotional pressure. Though largely ignored by metropolitan sports pages, and scorned by those who feel football is the "manly," American sport, soccer is booming at the grass roots level. Youth leagues are proliferating in cities such as Seattle, San Diego, Los Angeles, Dallas, St. Louis, Baltimore, Washington, D.C., and Miami, while the sport is challenging football for participatory interest (if not yet spectator appeal) in high schools and colleges everywhere. One day this enthusiasm should ensure an economic existence for the still-struggling North American Soccer League. But in the meantime the sport can thrive quite well on its own virtues, without the lure of professional riches or the parallel push from parents eager for junior to become the American Pele. Following are several reasons for soccer's growing acceptance:

1. Soccer provides an opportunity for the average-sized youngster who isn't particularly tall or heavy or strong, but who likes sports and wants to compete. Success at every level of soccer is a degree of skills, ability, and practice, not size. Whereas in sports like football, baseball, and basketball— except in specialized positions such as wide receiver, second base, or guard—those athletes under six feet are gradually being eliminated.

2. The nature of the game means there are fewer heroes, but also fewer bums. Play goes so fast, constantly flowing up and down and across the field, that mistakes are forgotten almost instantly. Explained Paul Saylor, a Los Angeles enthusiast who had played the game since he was a little boy on the East Coast, and whose son was now playing: "The football hero is the halfback who can run 60 yards for the touchdown. In soccer there is no physical way you can get the ball more than 10 yards without passing to a teammate. It's a team sport all the way." Ray Wells, a Miami soccer official added:

The boys who are linemen in football are ready to quit after the first year. They never saw the ball all year, they just stood there and hit somebody. But they love soccer because everybody gets a chance to be a quarterback. When they get the ball, they have to decide what to do with it. They have to make the attack and defend at all times. In football, there are only two or three who get all the glory and the rest of them just beat their brains out.

3. Schools and service clubs are increasingly attracted to the sport because of the low cost in fielding a team as compared to football, hockey, and baseball. A well-run soccer program will average barely ten dollars a boy, which includes uniforms, soccer balls, equipment to line the field, insurance, and referees. Youngsters can buy the cleats and the shin pads but they don't really need them; a pair of tennis sneakers, shorts, and a T-shirt will suffice. This, of course, is a major reason why soccer is the national sport in approximately 125 countries. Until recent years Americans haven't even been involved in the world's greatest sport.

4. In some areas, soccer fills a lapse in activity for many youngsters between the end of football and the beginning of baseball. This is especially true for those youngsters who are too small and uncoordinated for basketball or who don't enjoy the roughhouse elements and the crazy hours in hockey, if indeed the sport is available.

5. Soccer can be played successfully by boys and girls who are seven or eight, whereas their hand development and coordination for a sport like basketball doesn't really come until ten or eleven.

6. With action nearly continuous and free-flowing, soccer requires more individual imagination than a sport like football. Barring an Americanization of the rules, it seems impervious to a lot of coaching interference, one of the unpleasant aspects of other youth sports. Perhaps the foremost recommendations for soccer are the safety factors and the physical conditioning benefits. Mothers especially seem to understand the safety of the game. They see their youngsters working hard physically, running up and down the field against an opponent, but using finesse rather than the direct collision tactics of football and hockey. There is plenty of contact, of course, resulting in cuts and bruises, sore muscles, and twisted ankles, but more in the vein of basketball, where contact is brief under the basket in the fight for rebounds. Since the action seldom stops in soccer, it provides excellent aerobic exercise. Parents can watch their

youngster run, jump, kick, dive, and be constantly in motion, as opposed to baseball, where the big exercise is trotting back and forth to one's position each inning, chasing fly balls and base hits, and perhaps getting on base once or twice a game. In soccer, especially under enlightened American Youth Soccer Organization rules, which ensure that every youngster plays at least half the game, everybody is going to be tired out at the end, win or lose. The sport *requires* stamina if played correctly, and the youngster will be in shape to play any other sport.

(The American Youth Soccer Organization, with headquarters in Torrance, California, has over 4,000 teams in California, Hawaii, Oregon, Arizona, Utah, Kansas, Michigan, and Connecticut. Its motto is "Everybody Plays," and it has a rule to try to prevent dynasty building within its leagues. At the end of each season the top players from each team are shifted to other teams in their immediate area to keep the competition balanced.)

Despite all these arguments in its favor, soccer still finds itself on the defensive in this country. People within the sport must fight a complex about being "that other sport" and the feeling that they are serving as the dumping ground for those youngsters who can't cut it in football—"Why don't you try soccer, kid?" As British writer Hugh McIllvanney noted in *Sports Illustrated*: "The American public has been persistently wrong about soccer, so wrong that the most imaginative, fluent and graceful ball game ever devised is still laboring for a foothold in a country where sport is almost a surrogate religion."

Parents are generally the biggest obstacle to the Americanization of soccer. They grew up with football and baseball, and the notion that their youngster would naturally want to emulate a Joe Namath or a Sandy Koufax, and not some "foreigner" in a foreign sport. Some fathers will try to shame their sons out of playing soccer, insulted if they prefer to go out in the backyard and kick the ball around rather than play catch or throw the football. There is also the problem of securing qualified, interested coaches (as one Chicago cynic noted, "To say that you've developed a great soccer player, what does that get you?") and sufficient playing fields to meet the demand. Most fields are controlled by recreation and park officials, who traditionally favor football, or by the high school football coaches, who are already sensitive to the inroads being made by soccer. Thus many fields are reserved for Pop Warner football on weekends, relegating soccer to baseball diamonds and the like. The fact that soccer can adapt to any type of field is, of course, one of its great virtues.

Obviously, before the American public will take soccer to its heart, at least on the adult level, the sport must produce colorful personalities and eventually a national team that can reach the finals in World Cup competition. Fortunately, the sport's first American-born hero is a clean-cut, well-adjusted example for all young athletes. He is Kyle Rote, Jr., son of the former professional football player and a high-scoring center forward for the Dallas Tornados. Yet Rote had to come by his nationwide recognition through his surprising victory in the 1974 Superstars competition in Florida, where he pocketed $53,400 in a ten-sport duel with such athletic notables as Bob Seagren, Pete Rose, John Havlicek, Stan Smith, and O. J. Simpson. Overnight, soccer's new spokesman in this country turned out to be a ministerial student, married, and earning $1,400 a year as a pro, who emphasized that the money would bring no change in his life-style. "We'll pay a few bills, stash some away, share with those in need and try to be good stewards with the rest," said 6-foot, 185-pound Rote, who then added, "I hope now that people realize soccer isn't just a catch-all for the guys who are too small to play football."

He continued: "I hope the soccer players don't have the influence on kids that other athletes do. I hope that people see me as a regular guy who happened to be blessed with athletic ability. I'm on the podium to take the God-image out of athletics. You know, hero-worshipping is fine, as long as it doesn't get carried to the point where a kid says, 'If I'm not like so-and-so I'm a failure.' I hope people realize that a concert pianist and the guy pumping gas have the same relative value I have. . . . The saddest thing is to see a boy who has ability in another field being pushed into athletics by his dad. I was very lucky in that respect in that I was never pressured."

And so the goal in soccer is somehow to produce a teamful of Kyle Rote, Jr.'s who can one day win the World Cup. Setting high goals for the sport is fine, and certainly in keeping with the American competitive spirit. But the danger is that those who run youth soccer, those who coach it, and the parent spectators will succumb to the syndrome that often betrays the ideals of Pop Warner football, Little League baseball, and youth hockey. There is already evidence of this in hotbed areas where the game is growing so fast that it is outstripping football in the number of participants. Yet still, in general, soccer isn't played for the benefit of parental ego, or to fulfill a role in society. It is played by youngsters, and run by adults, who simply love the game for what it offers on the field. There's not the stress on winning, the gnashing of teeth when the best players aren't in the game, or the driving out of those who are too weak or too slow or too uncoordinated. That is why the sport is enjoying such robust growth, and why it must somehow withstand the rabid parents who will swarm to it once the financial rewards and public acclaim are there for everyone to see. When this happens, "Winning is everything" and his traveling companion "We're number one!" can't be far behind.

Epilogue: The Young Athlete's Bill of Rights

OUTSIDE OF THE FAMILY environment there's not a single area of activity that can influence a child's mental and physical development more than an involvement in sports. Humanistically approached, sensitively coached, and properly played, sports can develop a healthy body and a love for physical activity; they can instill the need for self-discipline and an appreciation for working hard to achieve one's goals; they can foster self-confidence and a feeling of worthwhileness; they can open up horizons, build close friendships, and nurture a meaningful respect for authority; team sports can teach the child about cooperation and working with others towards a common goal. Studies show that when a person gets involved in physical activity, his personality changes. He or she becomes more confident, more outgoing, and more sociable, with a corresponding release of aggression and tension as a result of this physical involvement.

Yet as I have reiterated throughout this book, these potential virtues of sports participation are being undermined by our

230

win-or-else, success-oriented approach to competition—most destructively at the preadolescent level. This is a period in every child's life when he is free. He wants to experiment with his capabilities; he wants to find himself. But if he turns to organized sports, he can find himself pressed down by rules and regulations and a life-and-death seriousness where he hoped to find loose, light-hearted leisure activities. The child is looking for self-identification, but instead he gets a "big league manager" shouting at him and harping on his mistakes and his weaknesses. He needs warmth and understanding, but instead he is lectured about the need to be tough and to "shake off" defeat, personal miscues, and minor injuries.

. But what can be done? Organized sports for children have become so ingrained in our society that we are unlikely ever to return to the laissez-faire, sandlot days when a piece of cardboard was second base and T-shirts marked the end zone. For one thing, too many high school coaches rely on the yearly influx of athletes who have been groomed at the Pop Warner–Little League level; these coaches aren't likely to leave this development to chance. Parents, meanwhile, are led to believe that unless their children start participating in sports at the earliest possible age, they will never be able to catch up in high school. And so everywhere, in cities and suburbs and small towns, leagues are organized by adults to feed this "need" for organized sports activity.

Yet who represents the child in all these maneuverings to mold miniature professionals? Nobody, really, except where enlightened parents or coaches back up a child's effort and involvement in a sport, regardless of the success attained. Otherwise the child is on his own, trying to cope with the pressures of competition, while adults try to rationalize the situation by arguing, "This is what kids want. They love sports." In view of the child's dilemma, if parents and coaches are going to continue to organize and run these leagues and laden them with their competitive fervor, then young athletes obviously need a voice on their own behalf. They need their own Athletic Bill of Rights to set guidelines for the attitudes and approaches taken by those in charge, at home and in their sport. The child should have:

1. The right to determine when to participate, and in what sport, and to what degree of intensity and involvement. This includes the freedom to quit a sport without being humiliated or otherwise punished by the parents. To take these decisions away from the child is to subject him to a dictatorship, which is a poor model for later life. Instead, the parents can spur the child's emotional growth by letting him make the final decisions, while offering support for those decisions.

2. The right to play in every game, no matter what his degree of physical ability or the relative "importance" of the game in terms of league competition. The child who doesn't get a chance to play is being told, in essence, that he's not worthwhile, and this can have a damaging effect on his personality. Similarly, leagues should attempt to ensure a sensible competitive level, i.e., with youngsters competing who are of similar size and ability.

3. The right to be taught the fundamentals of the sport by a qualified teacher-coach, and to play on fields, courts, and rinks that have been adjusted proportionally to children.

4. The right to be coached by those who have been trained or who have been made aware of the various stages of emotional and psychological development in children, and to be treated on a level equivalent to his emotional and physical maturity—not by the standards of collegiate or professional sports.

5. The right to have a coach who places him (the child) first, the team second, himself third, and winning fourth; to feel free to laugh after a defeat and to have fun participating even while playing on a losing team; to be able to use play as an opportunity to "try out" life, free of adult-imposed pressures to be a winner.

6. The right to have a coach who is patient and supportive, as opposed to one who believes in a harsh, negative, "profes-

sional" approach; a coach who takes time to work with each athlete, irrespective of ability or potential, and who offers periodic evaluation of the child's physical improvement and emotional growth as the season progresses.

7. The right to be treated as a member of a democracy, not a dictatorship, including the freedom to voice opinions openly to the coach without fear of repercussion. The coach who encourages his athletes to ask questions about technique or strategy, and to voice any personal dissatisfaction (e.g., lack of playing time or a dislike for the position one is playing) will maximize the youngster's growth process in the sport.

8. The right to proper medical treatment and supervision, including preseason and postseason physical exams, the close availability of a medically trained person at every practice and athletic contest, and proper protective equipment which has had demonstrated results via pretesting and which is checked regularly.

9. The right to report any physical pain to the coach and the parents without fear of ridicule or a loss of esteem. The child's complaint should be taken seriously, and there should be a medical examination. The child should be forbidden to participate until medical clearance has been obtained, to prevent coaches as well as parents from subjecting the child to further injuries, which may have long-range effects.

10. The right to freedom from physical and emotional punishment by the parents and by the coach. Punishment leads only to fear and constriction of behavior, whereas the purpose of sports should be to help a child grow, feel expansive, and realize his or her potential.

Index